fresh

First published in 2000 by New Holland Publishers (NZ) Ltd
Auckland • Sydney • London • Cape Town

218 Lake Road, Northcote, Auckland, New Zealand
14 Aquatic Drive, Frenchs Forest, NSW 2086, Australia
24 Nutford Place, London W1H 6DQ, United Kingdom
80 McKenzie Street, Cape Town 8001, South Africa

Copyright © 2000 in text: Julie Biuso
Copyright © 2000 in photography: Ian Batchelor
Copyright © 2000 New Holland Publishers (NZ) Ltd

Author photograph: courtesy *New Zealand Herald*

ISBN: 1-877246-45-X

Managing editor: Renée Lang
Cover and design: Christine Hansen
Editor: Barbara Nielsen

10 9 8 7 6 5 4 3 2 1

Printed through Phoenix Offset, Hong Kong

fresh

Julie Biuso

Photography by Ian Batchelor

NEW HOLLAND

cont

ents

To my father and mother

My love of vegetables, fresh from the garden, was instilled in me by my mother and my father. Dad grew them and Mum turned them into delicious dishes. I'm so sorry she's not here now, but Dad sure is. Although he's hitting 90, he cooks incredible meals for himself. He throws all the vegetables in one pot because it saves on washing up! But I'm so proud of him – so proud that he still grows his own carrots and beans, and amazing tomatoes and lettuces, and night after night, cooks up a one-pot storm in his own kitchen.

introduction

Food is more than fuel.
It's pleasure, it's passion,
it's sharing,
it's nourishing and nurturing,
all fused together in an orgasmic package.

Good food has always been important to me. I think it should titillate your tastebuds, nourish your body and soul and enhance your enjoyment of life. And vegetables, so often treated as merely an accompaniment, can do all these things and that's why I've made them the stars of the show in this book.

I'm not a killjoy; some butter, some cream, if it's mingling in the right company, is an acceptable treat, not a no-no. Balance is everything. I'm sure it's the key to a good life, maybe even a long life. The best advice, although it is clichéd, is to eat a varied diet and that is my family's philosophy.

I didn't consider myself privileged in any way as I grew up. Like many families we grew a lot of the vegetables we needed. Our garden was like an extension of the kitchen – we only had to reach out to pluck a sun-warmed lemon off the tree or to grab a handful of fresh, nose-tingling mint. As a child I understood where our food came from. I saw it growing, then being prepared, and I smelled it cooking.

I want to know what's in the food I'm putting in my mouth and in the mouths of my family. Getting back in touch with the food you eat, finding out how it is grown, how it is transported and stored, are all important factors in the chain of good health and good taste.

But, most important of all, to ensure that you get all the inherent goodness and flavour, the food you buy must be FRESH.

arouse

nibble

tease

stimulate

start

tempt

juices

titillate

taste buds

peck at

entice *allure*

flow

Spaghettini with Vine-ripened Tomato Sauce

Barbecued Corn with Chilli Lime Butter

Crispy Bean Cakes with Chilli Lime Yoghurt Sauce

Avocado with Tomato and Lemon Basil Dressing

Cos Lettuce with Croûtes of Melting Brie

Linguine with Cashew Nut and Garlic Sauce

Golden Salsa

Zucchini, Walnut and Blue Cheese Salad

Smoked Fish Cakes with Avocado and Lime Dressing

Mamaliga with Grilled Feta Topping

Grilled Red Pepper Rolls

Leeks with Tarragon and Tomato Vinaigrette

la dolce vita
Spaghettini with Vine-ripened Tomato Sauce

SERVES 4

500g outdoor tomatoes
1 large clove garlic, crushed
2 tablespoons coarsely chopped flat leaf parsley
small handful tiny basil leaves
salt
2 tiny dried 'bird's eye' chillies, crushed
12 black olives, pitted and chopped
3 tablespoons extra virgin olive oil
400g spaghettini (or use spaghetti)

Skin the tomatoes, cut them in half and flick out the seeds. Cut out the cores and chop the flesh into tiny dice, then put the tomatoes in a sieve set over a bowl. Leave to drain for 1 hour. Transfer the tomatoes to a bowl and mix in the garlic, parsley, basil leaves, ½ teaspoon of salt, the crushed chillies, the olives and the extra virgin olive oil.

Meanwhile, cook the pasta in plenty of boiling, well-salted water until al dente. Drain and tip into a heated serving dish. Pour on the sauce and quickly toss together. Serve immediately.

The beauty of this dish is that it doesn't seem to matter whether it is served hot, hottish, at room temperature, or even chilled; there are not many pasta dishes that are so flexible – and, at a pinch, it's not bad the next day!

It's essential to use tomatoes with flavour – not watery ones – and, because the sauce is not cooked, it's a good opportunity to use an exquisite estate-bottled extra virgin olive oil.

For a change, fry a few prawns in saffron-flavoured oil and serve them on top of the pasta (the pasta is best served hot for this dish).

There are several ways to remove the skin from a tomato – here's my way. The idea is to heat the tomato in water so the contents swell. This makes the skin taut and causes it to split. Lower the tomato into a pan of boiling water and leave it for about 10 seconds. Lift out and transfer to a bowl of cold water (this stops the tomato cooking any further). If the tomato is still hard to peel, repeat the process.

shuck Barbecued Corn with Chilli Lime Butter

To cook the cobs in their husks, remove the silks first. Pull down the husks leaf by leaf, remove the silks, then rewrap the cob carefully; tie it with string if necessary. Soak the corn cobs in cold water for 15–30 minutes. Cook over hot coals for 15–30 minutes, turning often. The corn will steam and become tender, the moisture preventing burning, but, once the water has evaporated, the sugars will caramelise, and a rich, sweet flavour will develop. Alternatively, cook the corn cobs on a hot barbecue plate, basting with a little water from time to time. Serve with Chilli Lime Butter or with wedges of lime and salt.

Chilli Lime Butter

1 fresh hot red chilli, halved, deseeded and very
**   finely chopped**
grated rind of 2 limes
200g butter, softened
1 clove garlic, crushed

Mix all the ingredients together in a bowl, cover, and chill until required.

frisky
Crispy Bean Cakes with Chilli Lime Yoghurt Sauce

SERVES 6 AS A STARTER OR 4 AS A PART OF A LIGHT MEAL

2 x 300g cans of kidney beans
$\frac{1}{2}$ teaspoon Tabasco sauce or a chilli sauce of your
    choice
1 clove garlic, crushed
1 tablespoon chopped marjoram or 1 teaspoon
    dried marjoram
1 small red onion, finely chopped
1 roasted red pepper (capsicum), peeled, cored,
    deseeded then finely diced (see page 20) or,
    for speed, use a small can of diced 'capsicums',
    drained
1 egg, separated
$\frac{1}{4}$ teaspoon salt
$\frac{3}{4}$ cup fresh white breadcrumbs
$\frac{1}{4}$ cup dried breadcrumbs
75ml olive oil

Drain the beans in a sieve and rinse them well with cold water. Drain again, then transfer to a bowl. Mash gently with a large fork or squash with your hands (the most effective method), leaving the beans a little lumpy. Blend in the Tabasco sauce, garlic, marjoram, red onion, red pepper, egg yolk, salt and fresh breadcrumbs. The mixture can be prepared several hours ahead to this point.

Whip the egg white until soft peaks form, then fold it through the bean mixture. Put the dried breadcrumbs on a piece of kitchen paper and drop large spoonfuls of the bean mixture onto the breadcrumbs (one at a time). Shape into rough rounds using the sides of the paper, not your fingers (the mixture is very soft). Shape into 12 cakes and transfer to a plate.

Heat the oil until piping hot in a large frying pan over a medium-high heat, then drop in the bean cakes. Fry until golden brown on all sides turning carefully with two spoons. Transfer to a plate lined with absorbent kitchen paper, then transfer to a serving plate. Serve with Chilli Lime Yoghurt Sauce.

Sauce

2 limes
300ml plain yoghurt
2 tablespoons chopped mint, or use chopped
    coriander
1 fresh hot red chilli, halved, deseeded and very
    finely chopped

Peel the limes with a small serrated knife, removing all the white pith. Cut in between each piece of membrane to release the tiny lime fillets. Let them drop into a bowl as you prepare them. Mix the yoghurt, mint and chilli with the lime fillets and serve with the bean cakes.

These bean cakes *are sensational and meat-eaters and vegetarians alike wolf them down. Don't be alarmed at how soft the mixture is when shaping them – lumps and bumps and squidgy shapes are more appealing than uniform neatness!*

Crispy Bean Cakes with Chilli Lime Yoghurt Sauce

green cradle Avocado with

Tomato and Lemon Basil Dressing

SERVES 6 AS A STARTER

4 tablespoons extra virgin olive oil
3 spring onions, finely chopped
1 large clove garlic, crushed
1 teaspoon raw sugar
1 teaspoon tomato purée
$\frac{1}{2}$ teaspoon Maldon sea salt
freshly ground black pepper to taste
6 small outdoor tomatoes, skinned and finely
**   chopped**
1 tablespoon shredded lemon basil, plus whole
**   leaves to garnish (or use regular basil)**
zest of 1 orange
juice of 1–2 oranges (use the second orange to thin
**   the dressing to a pouring consistency)**
3 ripe but firm avocados

Put the oil, spring onions, garlic, raw sugar, tomato purée, salt and black pepper, along with 4 of the prepared tomatoes, in a saucepan. Stir, set over a medium heat and cook gently until pulpy, about 12 minutes.

Add the basil, orange zest and juice, then fold through the remaining tomatoes. Cool and set aside (the sauce can be prepared up to 12 hours in advance; cover and keep refrigerated).

When ready to serve the avocados, halve them, extract the stones and put half an avocado on each plate. Spoon the dressing over, filling the cavities and letting the excess dressing form a pool on the plate. Garnish with extra basil leaves and serve immediately.

Avocados blow apart any theory that food which feels smooth and velvety in the mouth must be wickedly rich and bad for you. They contain more protein and fat than any other fruit, but the fat is mostly what is known as the 'good' kind, monounsaturated. Nutritional experts have labelled the avocado 'nutrient-dense'. To qualify for this term a food must provide at least four essential nutrients in the same percentage as the calories it supplies. Avocados provide five essential nutrients in this proportion: Vitamins A, B6, C, folic acid and the mineral copper. They are a good source of energy, are easily digested (and therefore suitable for babies), and their high protein content makes them a valuable food for vegetarians. Half an avocado provides about the same number of calories as 25g butter (180 calories).

Avocado can be used as a spread on bread or toast in place of butter. A dollop of mashed avocado, or guacamole (chillied avocado dip), on top of a jacket-baked potato is superb in place of butter.

melting Cos Lettuce with Croûtes of Melting Brie

SERVES 4–6

2 large red peppers (capsicums)
1 cos lettuce, broken apart, washed and dried
2 tablespoons capers in salt (see notes below)
1 large clove garlic, crushed
2 tablespoons finely chopped parsley
1 teaspoon Dijon mustard
freshly ground black pepper to taste
1 tablespoon white wine vinegar
salt
4 tablespoons extra virgin olive oil
half a French loaf, sliced into thick rounds
225g brie, sliced into thick wedges

Preheat the oven to 210°C. Put the peppers on the oven rack and cook for about 20 minutes, turning occasionally with tongs, or until they are blistered and charred (a piece of aluminium foil underneath is a good idea to catch drips and, later, melting blobs of brie). Transfer to a plate and, when cool enough to handle, peel off the skins and slip out and discard the cores and seeds; reserve any juices in a bowl. Cut the peppers into strips.

Tear the lettuce into pieces and put in a bowl with the peppers.

Chop the capers finely and mix in a bowl with the garlic, parsley, mustard, black pepper, vinegar and pepper juices. Add a good sprinkling of salt, blend the oil in and transfer to a small pan.

Toast the bread slices on one side under a hot grill, then turn and top with the brie. Grill until melted.

Meanwhile, gently warm the dressing (don't boil it). Dish the salad onto plates, arrange the croûtes on top and pour the warm dressing over. Serve immediately.

This makes a great supper dish for four without being too substantial, or serve it as a light starter for six.

Capers are the unopened flower buds of a Mediterranean shrub. They are picked while still tightly clenched, dried in the sun, then layered in barrels with rock salt or with vinegar. It is this process which enhances their flavour. Capers packed in salt will have a truer caper flavour; vinegar can overpower the taste. If buying capers packed in salt, check that the salt is white and not yellowing (yellowing is an indication of age). Wash off loose salt before using, and soak the capers in several changes of warm water for 15–30 minutes or until they lose excess salt. If using capers in brine, always drain them well before using.

long tongues Linguine with Cashew Nut and Garlic Sauce

SERVES 4

400g linguine (or use tagliatelle or fettuccine)
salt
$\frac{1}{2}$ cup plus 1 tablespoon extra virgin olive oil
150g salted cashew nuts, finely chopped
6 cloves garlic, crushed
freshly ground black pepper to taste
1 cup basil leaves, chopped
freshly grated Italian parmesan cheese for serving

Cook the pasta in plenty of gently boiling, well-salted water until al dente.

While the pasta is cooking, make the sauce. Put the $\frac{1}{2}$ cup of oil in a large frying pan. Add the cashews, garlic, $\frac{1}{4}$ teaspoon of salt and some black pepper. Heat gently.

When the linguine is ready, drain it and turn it into a heated serving bowl. Toss the tablespoon of oil and the basil through, then tip the cashew sauce over the top. Toss and serve immediately with parmesan.

honey & lime
Golden Salsa

SERVES 6–8

1 tablespoon liquid honey
juice of 1 lime
2 fresh hot red chillies, halved, deseeded and very
finely chopped
2 tablespoons shredded lemon or lime basil, or use
mint
6 golden kiwifruit, peeled and finely chopped

Mix the honey, lime juice, chillies and chosen herb in a bowl and add the golden kiwifruit. Marinate for 30 minutes before serving.

Golden kiwifruit *was developed in New Zealand. It has the same sunburst pattern as green kiwifruit, with a pale core around which dance a circle of tiny ruby-coloured seeds, and lemony yellow-coloured flesh. It doesn't have the nostril-clearing perfume or biting freshness of its green cousin. What it has is oodles of sweet tropical-fruit, melon and honey flavours, with a little ginger-beery zing. It's juicy and sweet but not cloying. And it's hairless.*

Included in its riches is a megadose of Vitamin C – one golden kiwifruit contains more than double the recommended daily intake of Vitamin C (Vitamin C is the first line of defence against cell-damaging free radicals). It is also rich in Vitamin E, which helps boost your immune system when you're stressed out or tired, and has no fats. There's probably no better piece of fruit to consume the morning after a night on the tiles!

This salsa is *stunning with avocado, either spooned into the hollows of halved avocados, or as a dressing on an avocado and chicken salad. It is also excellent as a salsa with whole baked or barbecued fish, fish kebabs or panfried or 'wokked' prawns. Spooned into tacos, on top of a refried bean mash (soften thickly sliced red onion in olive oil, mix in beans, cook until hot), shredded iceberg lettuce, sliced avocado and crisp, hot bacon, it is a revelation!*

slivers Zucchini, Walnut
and Blue Cheese Salad

SERVES 4

4–6 zucchini (courgettes), green or yellow or a
mixture
1½ tablespoons lemon juice
1 teaspoon liquid honey
¼ teaspoon salt
1 teaspoon chopped fresh marjoram, or more to
taste (I love marjoram and usually end up
putting more in this salad)
3 tablespoons walnut oil
100g soft creamy blue cheese, cut into triangles or
smallish pieces
2 tablespoons coarsely chopped walnuts
freshly ground black pepper to taste

Trim the ends of the zucchini, then use a potato peeler to shave off long slivers lengthways from each one (there will be a small amount of wastage; either chop it finely and add to the salad or use it in an Italian frittata or soup). Transfer the zucchini slivers to a bowl; if you are preparing them ahead of time, keep them covered and refrigerated.

Blend the lemon juice, honey, salt and marjoram together in a small bowl. Whisk in the oil.

When ready to serve, reblend the dressing and pour it over the zucchini. Toss gently, then top with the pieces of cheese and chopped walnuts. Grind on some black pepper, then serve immediately.

Whoever first put *blue cheese and honey on a plate together deserves a medal. I don't know what made me team the two of them with walnuts, walnut oil, musky marjoram and slivers of zucchini...but it's a mind-stretching combination which gets tongues wagging, and it's so good!*

It should go without saying that the walnuts must be fresh and the oil of good quality.

moist Smoked Fish Cakes with Avocado and Lime Dressing

SERVES 6 AS A STARTER OR 4 AS A MAIN COURSE

500g (about 5 medium) even-sized waxy potatoes, washed but not peeled

salt

450g hot-smoked salmon or smoked fish of your choice (if using smoked fish which has a lot of bones, allow an extra 100g for the bones)

LIME DRESSING

2 fresh limes

$\frac{1}{4}$ teaspoon salt

3 tablespoons lemon-infused extra virgin olive oil (or use extra virgin olive oil)

1–2 fresh hot red chillies, halved, deseeded and very finely chopped

a few small fresh mint leaves

1 large onion, finely chopped

1 tablespoon butter

$\frac{1}{2}$ teaspoon salt

freshly ground black pepper to taste

1 egg

plain flour for dusting

oil for frying

2 ripe but firm avocados

Cook the unpeeled potatoes gently in salted water until they are nearly tender. Drain, then, when cool, refrigerate for several hours (if you try to grate them while they are warm, they'll go gluggy).

Remove any skin, scales and bones from the smoked fish. Flake the fish and put it in a china or glass bowl; the fish can be prepared several hours ahead but keep it covered and refrigerated.

Peel the limes with a small serrated knife, removing all the white pith. Cut in between each piece of membrane to release the tiny lime fillets. Let them drop into a bowl as they are cut free. Mix in the other dressing ingredients except the mint.

Put the onion in a pan with the butter, cover with a lid and cook gently until softened. Cool. Peel the potatoes, grate them and add them to the bowl of smoked fish. Mix in the cooled onion, $\frac{1}{2}$ teaspoon of salt, plenty of black pepper and the egg. Shape into large cakes, then dust lightly with flour.

Cook the fish cakes in hot oil in a large frying pan set over a medium heat. When they are golden all over, transfer them to a serving plate.

Meanwhile, peel the avocados, cut them into slices and arrange them around the fish cakes. Add the mint leaves to the dressing and spoon it over the avocado and fish cakes. Serve immediately.

These are the most incredible fish cakes I've ever tasted and are good made with most smoked fish but I'm currently hooked on hot-smoked salmon. Because salmon is an oily fish, it stays very moist when hot-smoked, unlike white-fleshed fish, which can easily become dry if not prepared with care. I advise you to choose large smoked fish because most smokehouses smoke the batches of fish to ensure that the largest ones are cured, usually at the expense of the smaller ones being overdone.

Back to the fish cakes. They're so light, barely held together by a smidgen of egg, with gratings of cooked potato, and onion cooked until soft and sweet in butter, letting the salmon flavour shine through. Extraordinary really! You have to treat them carefully when you shape and fry them because they're so light, but you should get the hang of it soon enough. The avocado and lime dressing brings the dish to a stunning climax.

The fish cake mixture can be made ahead, and shaped into cakes, but don't flour the cakes until you're ready to fry them.

Don't attempt the fish cakes with regular smoked salmon, which is not cooked but is cured by faintly warm smoke. Hot-smoked fish is partially or wholly cooked during the smoking process, the smoking being used to flavour the fish rather than to preserve it.

Smoked Fish Cakes with Avocado and Lime Dressing

drizzle Mamaliga with Grilled Feta Topping

SERVES 6 OR MORE AS A STARTER

1.25 litres water
1 teaspoon salt
250g coarse polenta
250g feta cheese, crumbled (choose a firm feta, not a soft, squishy one)
freshly ground black pepper to taste
dried oregano
60g butter
2 large cloves garlic, crushed

Bring the water to the boil in a large, wide (not tall and narrow) saucepan. Add the salt, then sprinkle in the polenta a handful at a time letting it fall through your fingers from a height, or tap it in from a bowl. Stir continuously, using a wooden spoon. If you add the polenta too fast, it will form lumps (if this happens, fish them out because they will not break down during cooking). Once all the polenta is added, turn the heat to low and cook gently for about 25 minutes, giving 3–4 good stirs every 20 seconds or so.

When the polenta is cooked (the wooden spoon will stay upright in the centre of the polenta), tip it onto a tray and spread out 1–1.5cm thick. Smooth the surface and leave to cool. The cooked polenta can be stored for several hours at room temperature and up to 2 days covered and refrigerated.

When you are ready to finish off the mamaliga, cut the polenta into squares and transfer it to a baking tray or trays. Distribute the feta over the top, grind on some black pepper and sprinkle on a little oregano. Bake in an oven preheated to 200°C for approximately 15 minutes or until the feta is a rich golden brown.

Meanwhile, melt the butter in a small saucepan and add the garlic. Continue to cook until the garlic turns a pale golden brown (be careful not to burn it). Transfer the mamaliga to a serving plate and drizzle the browned garlic butter over the top. Serve immediately with Grilled Red Pepper Rolls.

Instant Polenta
Regular polenta gives off a more pronounced corn aroma as it cooks and has a richer corn taste and 'gruntier' texture than instant polenta, but most people will find these differences hard to detect. If you're a purist, use regular polenta, which will take around 25 minutes to cook. But if you're a speedy cook, opt for the instant variety, which will cook in about 5 minutes.

Grilled Red Pepper Rolls

3 large red peppers (capsicums)
oil

STUFFING
large knob of butter
$\frac{1}{2}$ cup fresh breadcrumbs
1 small clove garlic, crushed
2 tablespoons finely chopped parsley
1 tablespoon capers, drained and chopped
a few pinches of salt
freshly ground black pepper to taste

Preheat the oven to 210°C. Put the peppers on the oven rack and cook for about 20 minutes, turning occasionally with tongs, or until they are blistered and charred. Transfer to a plate.

To make the stuffing, set a small frying pan over a medium-low heat and add the butter. Put in the breadcrumbs and cook gently until lightly browned, stirring often. Remove the pan from the heat and mix in the garlic, parsley, capers, salt and black pepper.

When the peppers are cool, peel off the skins and slip out and discard the cores and seeds. Cut the flesh into strips about 3cm wide. Put a small amount of the stuffing on two-thirds of each pepper strip. Roll up, starting from the end with the stuffing on it.

Put the pepper rolls in a shallow ovenproof dish. The peppers can be prepared several hours ahead to this point; cover and refrigerate. Before grilling or baking them, brush the peppers with oil, sprinkle over any remaining filling, then grill them until hot and lightly coloured; alternatively, warm them through in a hot oven.

__Mamaliga__ is a typical Romanian dish made of stone-ground cornmeal, similar to Italian polenta. It is served steaming hot, like polenta, or it can be fried or baked. I use Italian polenta in this recipe. Polenta was first brought to Italy from its native Mexico by the Venetians several centuries ago. It remains a staple food in the north of Italy, where several varieties are common, and it's also popular in Tuscany. It is standard fare in most Balkan countries too.

This dish can also be served as a main course for vegetarians – team it with a good salad or two.

Mamaliga with Grilled Feta Topping

grill  Leeks with Tarragon and Tomato Vinaigrette

SERVES 8

6 slim leeks, with roots intact (or 12 baby leeks)
1 tablespoon extra virgin olive oil
1 tablespoon walnut oil
grated zest of 1 lemon
salt
freshly ground black pepper to taste

DRESSING
1 large ripe tomato, skinned (see page 10)
1 teaspoon green peppercorns, drained
$\frac{1}{4}$ teaspoon salt
freshly ground black pepper to taste
1 teaspoon tarragon wine vinegar
$\frac{1}{2}$ teaspoon Dijon mustard
3 tablespoons extra virgin olive oil

Trim the leek tops, then remove coarse outer leaves. Trim the roots, taking care not to cut them off entirely, as they will hold the leeks together during cooking. Cut each leek in half lengthways, unless the leeks are very slim ones. Put the leeks in a dish long enough to accommodate them, drizzle with olive oil and walnut oil, add the lemon zest, sprinkle with a little salt and grind on some black pepper. Coat the leeks in the oil mixture.

Cook the leeks on a barbecue hot plate set on a medium-low heat. Once they soften and start to wilt, transfer them to the hot grill rack and cook until they are a rich, golden brown. Transfer them to a plate and pour the dressing on.

Dressing

Cut the tomato in half, scoop out the seeds and put the seeds in a small sieve set over a bowl. Extract as much juice as possible, then discard the seeds. Cut the tomato flesh into fine slivers, then cover and set aside.

When you are ready to serve, combine the green pepper-corns, salt, black pepper to taste, the vinegar, mustard, oil and tomato juice. Whisk well. Add the slivered tomato to the dressing, stir well and spoon over the leeks. Toss gently then serve.

These leeks can be served as a starter or as a vegetable accompaniment – they're particularly tasty with ham, chicken and veal dishes. Don't attempt the dish with huge leeks.

Leeks with Tarragon and Tomato Vinaigrette

germinate

pristine

sprout

live

blossom

tender

snap

tight buds

crisp

tease

bloom

newness

Asparagus Frittata

Sautéed Witloof

Sweet Peas

Roasted Fennel with Lemon

Potato and Asparagus Salad

Asparagus and Camembert Pies

Fennel Niçoise

Artichokes Roman-style

Baby Carrots and Turnips with Broad Beans

Glazed Fennel

shoots

spears Asparagus Frittata

SERVES 4

350g very slim asparagus spears
salt
5 eggs, at room temperature
freshly ground black pepper to taste
$\frac{1}{3}$ cup freshly grated Italian parmesan cheese
4–5 tablespoons olive oil

Trim the asparagus spears and wash them well. Plunge them into a saucepan of boiling, lightly salted water. Cook, uncovered, until very tender (don't undercook them; if they are crunchy, the frittata will break apart).

Break the eggs into a bowl and beat lightly with a fork. Add $\frac{1}{4}$ teaspoon of salt, some black pepper and the parmesan. Carefully blend in the whole asparagus spears.

Heat 4 tablespoons of the oil in a large, shallow frying pan over a medium-low heat. Pour in the asparagus mixture. Cook gently, until the bottom is golden brown, loosening the frittata from the sides and bottom of the pan as it cooks.

When it is nearly set on top, slip the whole thing out onto a plate. If the pan seems dry, add a little more oil and swirl it around. Cover the frittata with another plate, then invert so what was the top plate is now on the bottom (the idea is to be able to then slide the frittata back into the pan so that the nearly set part is now on the underside). Cook until the underside is set and golden. Slide onto a clean plate and serve hottish or warm.

Fat spears of asparagus are delicious dunked into melted butter or an olive oil dip, but it's best to use skinny ones for frittata; fat spears easily break up the slices when you cut the frittata. Skinny ones are also good in stirfries, because they cook more quickly.

I loathe frittata impostors – those great door-stopper wodges of soggy vegetables encased in too much firm dry egg. A frittata should be thin, really just a few seasonings flavouring the eggs, or slightly more substantial, with a few vegetables held together with eggs. It should never be made in a cake tin or roasting dish (that's a vegetable bake), nor should it be a home for last week's leftovers.

If you're nervous about the flipping business, lightly brown the top of the frittata under a hot grill. However, the best result is achieved by cooking both sides in hot oil in the pan because the oil flavours the frittata and makes it crisp; grilling can make the frittata dry and too firm.

white tips Sautéed Witloof

SERVES 4

strained juice of 1 lemon
salt
6–8 witloof (Belgian endive)
large knob of butter
freshly ground black pepper to taste
1 tablespoon finely chopped parsley

Bring a pot of water to the boil, add the lemon juice and $\frac{1}{2}$ teaspoon of salt. Plunge the witloof into the water, pushing them under the water to stop discolouration (don't be alarmed if they turn a mauvey brown colour). Cook for 3 minutes, drain and refresh generously with cold water. Trim the ends then shake out excess water. Chop coarsely.

Heat a frying pan over a medium-high heat and when it is hot, add the butter. When the butter is sizzling, add the witloof, increase the heat to high and stirfry for 7–10 minutes until browned. Season with a little more salt and some black pepper. Sprinkle the parsley over, turn into a heated dish and serve.

I adore witloof in a salad – it adds a juicy crunch and a bitter-sweet edge which is welcome at the end of a meal. Tree-ripened citrus fruit, especially oranges but also grapefruit, towards the end of their season (they're sweeter at this time), are superb with a salad of witloof and fresh walnuts, dressed with walnut oil and a smattering of fresh chervil or chives. See also Witloof, Watercress and Orange Salad (page 106).

Witloof translates as white leaf. In France it is called endive, and in Italy it is called cicoria. There is a delicious lettuce, a different vegetable altogether, which the French call chicory and the Italians call endivia. How confusing!

Witloof has juicy leaves with a hint of bitterness. If it is exposed to the light it will become very bitter – that's why it should be sold wrapped in light-resistant paper. Red-leaved witloof is gorgeous in a mixed salad – plump juicy leaves with a little bitterness. Witloof contains good quantities of Vitamin A, calcium, iron and potassium.

Witloof is an interesting vegetable to serve hot, too. Try it blanched whole as described, but cook it until nearly tender, then roll it in a hot pan with 'burnt' butter (butter cooked until browned and nutty-smelling). Finish off with a few squirts of lemon juice. A curious thing happens when you cook witloof like this, and in the main recipe – it tastes like artichokes!

french heart Sweet Peas

SERVES 4–6

1kg fresh peas in the pod (should yield about 3 cups shelled peas), or use 350g baby frozen peas
1 heart of a small buttercrunch (butter) lettuce, finely shredded (use the pale green or yellow leaves only)
salt
freshly ground black pepper to taste
½ teaspoon sugar
50g butter
½ cup fresh mint leaves

Put the peas in a saucepan with the lettuce, salt to taste, black pepper and sugar. Barely cover with cold water, then bring to the boil, uncovered, and cook until tender.

Frozen peas will take about 8 minutes, while fresh peas will take 15–20 minutes. Drain the peas and return them to the cleaned pan with the butter, and set back over a gentle heat until the butter melts, about 2–3 minutes. Chop the mint, add to the peas and serve.

pickled Roasted Fennel with Lemon

SERVES 4–6

3–4 medium fennel bulbs
1 tablespoon extra virgin olive oil
freshly ground black pepper to taste
2 pickled or preserved lemons
Kalamata olives
Italian Cerignola green olives or Spanish green olives

Trim the fennel bulbs then cut them into quarters through the root. Rub with the olive oil, put the fennel in a shallow ovenproof dish and grind on some black pepper. Bake for about 30 minutes in an oven preheated to 200°C, or until tender and lightly browned.

Rinse off the pulp from the pickled or preserved lemon rinds, then cut the pieces of rind into strips. Put the roasted fennel onto a serving plate and garnish with the lemon rind and olives.

Fennel must be fresh *and young for roasting because if there is not enough juiciness in the bulb it will be dry. The result when right is nothing short of sensational: charred extremes, juicy but al dente interior, enhanced aniseed flavour, rich oily taste – all blitzed by bursts of salt and lemon. Seaside stuff to be sure! Serve with fish, simply cooked, or for vegetarians serve with couscous and a garlicky spinach and yoghurt salad.*

Roasted Fennel with Lemon

spring fling

Potato and Asparagus Salad

SERVES 6

1kg waxy new potatoes, scrubbed
salt
1½ tablespoons white wine vinegar
freshly ground black pepper to taste
2 cloves garlic, crushed
100ml extra virgin olive oil
grated zest of 1 orange
3 tablespoons finely chopped herbs (mint, parsley, marjoram)
350g asparagus, trimmed and rinsed

Put the potatoes in a steaming basket or metal colander and set this over a saucepan of boiling water. Sprinkle with salt, cover with a lid or aluminium foil, set over a medium-high heat and steam for 20–30 minutes or until tender. Lift off the lid and remove the steaming basket from the saucepan.

In a small bowl blend the vinegar, ½ teaspoon of salt, some black pepper and the garlic, then whisk in the oil. Pour off about one-quarter of the dressing into a larger bowl and add the grated orange zest to it. Set this aside for the asparagus. Add the herbs to the small bowl of dressing and set it aside for the potatoes.

Slice the potatoes while they are still warm (if the skin is tough, peel the potatoes) and arrange them in a ring on a large, shallow dish. Pour the herby dressing over them.

Plunge the asparagus into a saucepan of boiling salted water and cook, uncovered, for 2–7 minutes or until crisp-tender. Drain and refresh with cold water. Drain briefly, then pat dry with absorbent kitchen paper. Cut the asparagus into short lengths, and tip them into the bowl of orange-flavoured dressing. Toss well, then pile this into the centre of the potato salad. Serve warmish or at room temperature.

Asparagus remains one of the true signs of spring. When it first appears there's no better way of serving it than with a puddle of extra virgin olive oil and a bowl of freshly grated Italian parmesan cheese to dunk it into or a bowl of just-melted garlic butter. As the season moves on you need to be more inventive. Rubbing the spears with a little olive oil and roasting them on high until the tips turn crispy and develop a caramelised flavour is always worth doing. The hint of orange in this salad, coupled with a fresh herb dressing on potatoes, makes a great salad. It's excellent with a thick slab of panfried ham-off-the-bone.

Potato and Asparagus Salad

spring tarts Asparagus and Camembert Pies

MAKES 10 TARTS

400g fat asparagus spears, trimmed
salt
3 spring onions, finely sliced
1 clove garlic, crushed
knob of butter
2 egg yolks
$\frac{1}{4}$ cup cream
$\frac{1}{2}$ cup fresh white breadcrumbs
150g camembert cheese, cubed (leave rind on)
good grating of fresh nutmeg
freshly grated black pepper to taste
5 sheets (750g) purchased ready-rolled puff pastry,
**   thawed**
1 egg, beaten with a pinch of salt

Plunge the asparagus into a saucepan of boiling, lightly salted water. Cook, uncovered, for 1 minute. Drain, refresh with cold water, then leave to drain again. Pat dry with absorbent kitchen paper, then cut into short lengths.

Put the spring onions and garlic in a saucepan with the butter. Cover and cook over a low heat until soft. Mix the egg yolks and cream together in a bowl and add the asparagus, cooled spring onion mixture, breadcrumbs, cheese, a generous $\frac{1}{4}$ teaspoon of salt, and nutmeg and black pepper to taste.

Meanwhile, cut from the pastry sheets ten rounds approximately 10.5cm in diameter and another ten rounds approx 11.5cm in diameter. Prick the bases of the smaller rounds with a fork and dab the edges with a little cold water. Spoon the filling onto these pastry rounds, mounding it up and keeping it in from the edges. Put the larger rounds of pastry on top and gently press the edges of the pastry rounds together to seal. Use a small knife to 'knock the edges up' (see following).

Make a decorative border by marking vertical indentations on the edges of the dough. Cut a small hole in the centre of each tart to allow steam to escape; this stops the pastry becoming soggy. Use the knife to mark a lattice pattern on top of each tart. If the pastry is soft, refrigerate the pies for 30 minutes.

Brush with beaten egg and bake in the top third of an oven preheated to 225°C for 15 minutes or until well-browned and crisp. Serve hot.

Knocking Up Pastry Edges

This means to make light horizontal indentations along the edges of the pastry seam with a small sharp knife. If the edges of the pastry are pressed too hard or squashed during shaping, or gummed up with egg wash, the pastry cannot rise properly. By loosening the extreme edges, without breaking the seal, the pastry can live up to its name of 'puff' pastry and puff up.

These pies take a little bit of work, but they can be prepared a few hours before cooking (cover with plastic food wrap and refrigerate). A fruity salad, with buttercrunch lettuce, black grapes and sliced juicy ripe pear, dressed with a tarragon vinegar, extra virgin olive oil and a dash of walnut oil dressing, is a great accompaniment. It makes a special all-vegetable main course.

nice Fennel Niçoise

SERVES 6

4 fennel bulbs (about 1.2kg)
5 tablespoons extra virgin olive oil
1 large onion, finely sliced
2 cloves garlic, finely chopped
400g can Italian tomatoes, mashed
$\frac{1}{4}$ teaspoon salt
1 tablespoon finely chopped marjoram (or use
  $\frac{1}{2}$ teaspoon dried marjoram)
2 fresh bay leaves
freshly ground black pepper to taste
$\frac{1}{2}$ cup Kalamata olives
2 tablespoons chopped flat leaf parsley

Prepare the fennel by trimming away the root ends, removing stems and any bruised or coarse parts. Wash well, then slice into thick wedges.

Put 2 tablespoons of the oil in a medium-sized saucepan and set on a low heat. Add the onion and garlic, cover with a lid and cook gently until softened (about 10 minutes). Transfer to a plate and add the rest of the oil to the saucepan. Increase the heat to medium-high and add the fennel. Cook, uncovered, for about 10 minutes, stirring often, or until lightly browned.

Return the onion and garlic to the pan and add the tomatoes, salt, marjoram, bay leaves and black pepper. Stir well to combine the ingredients, then bring to the boil. Simmer uncovered for 15–30 minutes or until tender (depends on the maturity of the fennel). Mix in the olives and parsley. Serve hot or at room temperature.

The herb fennel *has many culinary uses. The leaves can be used fresh and the stems can be dried and set alight under a barbecued fish to impart a smoky flavour.*

'Florence' fennel (often called by its Italian name 'finocchio') forms a swollen stem underground. Referred to as a bulb, it is white, and crisp like celery, but with a distinctive aniseed flavour. When fresh and crisp it can be eaten raw, dunked into a vinaigrette or sliced and used in salads. It also makes an excellent cooked vegetable. It can be crumbed and fried, stewed, sauced, sautéed, roasted and barbecued. Cooking it mutes its aniseedy flavour, making it taste more like celery.

Fennel seeds are different again. Although native to the Mediterranean, fennel is a common spice in Indian cookery. The seeds are aromatic and taste of sweet hay with just a little pungency. Their most reputed use is as an aid to digestion. In India the seeds are eaten raw after a meal as a digestive. In Italy fennel seeds are often teamed with pork dishes, as pork takes longer to digest than most other meats. The seeds can be used in sweet and savoury dishes.

Fennel Niçoise

bottoms up

Artichokes Roman-style

SERVES 4

4 large globe artichokes with stems attached
juice of 1 lemon mixed with 2 litres water
2 large cloves garlic, peeled and finely chopped
2 tablespoons finely chopped mint
$\frac{1}{2}$ teaspoon salt, or to taste
freshly ground black pepper to taste
3 tablespoons finely chopped parsley
$\frac{1}{4}$ cup extra virgin olive oil

Prepare as described for stuffed artichokes (see notes following). As the artichokes are prepared, plunge them into the acidulated water.

In a bowl mix the garlic, mint, salt, black pepper and parsley. Set aside one third of this mixture and press the rest into the cavities of the artichokes.

Choose a heavy-based casserole just large enough to contain the artichokes. Put the artichokes in the casserole with stems pointing up. Smear the rest of the herb mixture over the outside of the artichokes. Drizzle the oil over and add enough water to come about one-third of the way up the leaves. Put on a lid and cook over a medium heat for 30–40 minutes or until tender and easily pierced by a skewer; check regularly and don't overcook.

Transfer the artichokes to a serving dish, arranging them with the stems up. If the juices in the pan are on the thin side, simply reduce them over a high heat until an emulsion forms between the oil and the water, then pour the juices over the artichokes.

Roman food is gutsy and sensual – as this superb treatment for globe artichokes shows (even enormous varieties are made tender and palatable by this method). Don't waste the stems, they're edible too, but have an earthier taste than the leaves.

The globe artichoke is a type of thistle. The flower buds are the bits which are eaten and they are edible at various stages of their growth, but are better picked and eaten while young. If they are left on the plant the thistles develop and turn into a striking flower which can be dried and used in flower arrangements.

If you grow your own globe artichokes, they can be picked when they are very small, trimmed, and eaten raw, dressed with just a trickle of fine extra virgin olive oil and a squeeze of lemon juice. They are a nutty-tasting treat. They are also delicious doused in olive oil and lightly grilled.

If the artichokes are more mature, they can be boiled or steamed and finished off in a number of ways.

There are several ways to prepare an artichoke. First, fill a bowl with water and squeeze the juice of a lemon into it. As the artichokes are prepared, put them in the acidulated water; the lemon will help prevent them discolouring. It's a good idea to wear thin food-preparation gloves when preparing artichokes to prevent them staining your hands.

Cut off the top third of the artichoke and discard (the tips of the leaves are not edible). Trim the stalk; if it is fibrous, peel the outside of it. The artichoke can be boiled as it is and the choke removed after cooking. This is suitable when artichokes are to be served cold.

If you want to cook the artichokes with seasoning or stuffing, trim off the top third of the leaves, then spread the leaves apart, opening and loosening the trimmed artichoke. Remove the mauve-coloured leaves in the centre, then press the soft, yellowish leaves away from the centre until a cavity is formed and the choke is revealed. The choke is a collection of fibrous hairs, which should be totally scraped out as it is inedible, even after cooking. Use a pointed teaspoon to remove it, but take care to remove only the hairy fibre, because directly below this is the meaty base of the artichoke (referred to as the fond or heart). The artichoke is then ready for seasoning or stuffing.

If the artichokes are to be sliced, it is easier to cut off the tips, slice the artichokes in half and extract the choke from each half before slicing.

mere babes Baby Carrots and Turnips with Broad Beans

SERVES 4

1kg fresh broad beans or 500g frozen broad beans
salt
1–2 bunches (about 600g, trimmed) baby carrots,
**   trimmed, washed and peeled**
1 bunch baby turnips, trimmed, washed and
**   peeled**
knob of butter
grated zest of 1 lemon
knob of grated ginger
50ml chicken stock, possibly a little more
freshly ground black pepper to taste

Remove the broad beans from their pods, then drop them into a saucepan of boiling, lightly salted water. Bring the water back to the boil, then cook the beans for 5–7 minutes. If using frozen broad beans, cook for 3 minutes only or until piping hot. Drain, refresh with cold water and drain again. When cool enough to handle, remove the tough outer skins (fiddly but necessary). Set aside.

Put the carrots in a saucepan with salted water and bring to the boil. Cook gently for 2–5 minutes, depending on their size, then drain and refresh with cold water. Repeat the process with the turnips. The vegetables can be prepared 1–2 hours in advance.

Put the butter in a large frying pan with the lemon zest. Squeeze the juice from the grated ginger directly into the pan and add the chicken stock, a few pinches of salt and some black pepper. Add the vegetables. Bring to a gentle boil and cook for a few minutes, until piping hot, stirring occasionally. Turn into a heated serving dish and serve immediately.

buttered Glazed Fennel

SERVES 4

4 slim bulbs of fennel
salt
juice of $\frac{1}{2}$ a lemon
large knob of butter
1 tablespoon finely chopped fennel leaves
**   (optional)**
freshly ground black pepper to taste

Prepare the fennel by trimming away the root end and removing stems and any bruised or coarse parts. Wash well. Plunge into a saucepan of boiling, lightly salted water, add the lemon juice and cook, uncovered, at a gentle boil for 15–20 minutes or until tender. (Check with a skewer; be careful not to overcook them.)

Drain, refresh with cold water, shake out excess water and drain for 1–2 minutes.

Return the fennel to the pan with the butter, set it over a low heat and allow it to heat through until it is very lightly browned. Sprinkle the fennel leaves on, if using, and grind on some black pepper. Tip the fennel into a heated serving dish and serve immediately.

health

well

resuscitate

revi

goodness

renew

reawaken

rouse

being

nutrients

restore

ve

Spinach Florentine

Brazilian Turtle Soup

Roesti

Piperade

Mushroom-filled Brioche

Huevos con Chorizo

refresh

inspire

translucent Spinach Florentine

SERVES 4–6

**6 large very fresh free-range eggs, at room
   temperature**
50g butter
2 x 400g bunches spinach, trimmed and washed
salt
freshly ground black pepper to taste
freshly grated nutmeg to taste
**50g piece Italian parmesan cheese, very thinly
   sliced**
2 tablespoons cream

Here is a foolproof way to poach eggs. Fill a large frying pan with hot water and set over a high heat. Bring the water to just under boiling point. Break the eggs into a dish, swirl the water, carefully lower the eggs into the water, cover the pan with a lid and remove the pan from the heat. Leave it for 10 minutes, during which time the egg whites should set, but the yolks should still be runny. Check the firmness of the eggs after 6 minutes to make sure they are not becoming firm too quickly – remove from the water when they are ready. If the eggs aren't ready after 10 minutes, leave them until they are done.

If you want to prepare the eggs up to an hour in advance, cook them as described and transfer to a shallow dish of cold water until required.

Meanwhile, heat a large heavy-based frying pan over a high heat. When it is hot, drop in a knob of butter. As soon as it melts, throw in a quarter of the spinach. Turn continuously until the spinach wilts, seasoning each batch with salt, black pepper and nutmeg, then transfer it to a large colander. If the pan is dry, add another knob of butter and repeat the process (if water accumulates in the pan, tip it off).

Continue cooking the spinach this way. Press the spinach lightly, then form it into six 'nests' on a chopping board. Put the nests of spinach in a buttered shallow ovenproof dish. When the eggs are ready, lift them carefully out of the water one at a time with a slotted spoon (they will be very delicate), mop underneath them with absorbent kitchen paper to soak up any water, then place them in the spinach nests. Drape the parmesan over the eggs and spoon the cream over. Glaze under a hot grill for 2–3 minutes or until the cheese is golden. Serve immediately, with crusty bread, for a brunch or light supper dish.

To poach eggs successfully, they need to be very fresh. The egg white of a fresh egg clings to the yolk, making it hard to separate the two, so you get a neat little bundle of cooked egg white nestling around the yolk when you poach the egg. As the egg ages, the white thins and becomes less gelatinous. In the extreme, the egg white will disintegrate in the poaching water. As a precaution, some cooks add a teaspoon of vinegar to the poaching water (it does give the eggs a slight tang), which helps the egg white set. It is best to use very fresh eggs for frying too, so that you end up with a plump yolk surrounded by a ring of egg white. However, when it comes to hard-boiled eggs, a little age is a good thing (see page 66).

Leafy vegetables like spinach can be cooked with just the water left clinging to them after washing. Put them in a saucepan, set over a medium heat and stir the spinach often until it has wilted or is cooked to your liking. Salt added to the spinach as it cooks will minimise the chalky taste it sometimes has.

Spinach Florentine

slow Brazilian Turtle Soup

SERVES 6–8

500g (approximately 2½ cups) black turtle beans
1 bacon hock (700–800g)
2 tablespoons olive oil
1 onion, chopped
4 cloves garlic, crushed
1 tablespoon ground cumin
pinch of chilli powder
3.5 litres water
2 fresh bay leaves
freshly ground black pepper to taste
2 tablespoons flat leaf parsley
salt
1 tablespoon fresh lime juice
1 red pepper (capsicum), halved, cored and sliced
2 tablespoons chopped coriander

GARNISH
sour cream
sliced red pepper (capsicum)
chopped coriander
lime zest

Rinse the beans well and soak them overnight in cold water to cover. Drain, rinse and drain again. Rinse the bacon hock, then soak it in cold water for 30 minutes.

Heat the oil in a large saucepan over a low heat and add the onion and garlic. Cook gently for about 10 minutes, until the onion is soft but not coloured. Stir in the ground cumin and chilli powder and cook for a minute. Add the beans, the water, the drained bacon hock, bay leaves and black pepper. Bring to the boil, skim well, then add the parsley. Lower the heat and cook gently, uncovered, for 2–2½ hours or until the beans are very tender and the liquid is reduced by one-third.

Remove the bacon hock to a board and when it is cool enough to handle, peel off the skin and shred the meat, discarding any fatty pieces or sinew. Return the meat to the soup and add 1 teaspoon of salt, the lime juice, red pepper and coriander. Cook for 15 minutes more, check for seasoning (don't be surprised if you need more salt), then ladle into soup bowls. Garnish each bowl with a blob of sour cream, a few slices of red pepper, a little chopped coriander and a couple of peels of lime zest. Serve immediately.

Brazilian Turtle Soup

__This dark, mysterious brew__ is extraordinary – you can almost feel the life flow through your veins as you eat it.

The garnish is important – the spiciness of the dish is muted with a dollop of sour cream, the rich earthy beans are freshened with a squirt of lime and the whole is sweetened with red pepper.

If a bacon hock is not available, use a fresh pork hock, but increase the salt to 2 teaspoons.

Serve this soup as a main course, with beers and coarse wholegrain or black bread.

__Slow Food__ is the perfect antidote to today's fast food syndrome. The movement was founded in Italy in 1986 by Carlo Petrini in response to the opening of the first McDonald's restaurant in Piazza di Spagna in Rome. The principles of Slow Food are to uphold or rediscover authentic culinary traditions and the conservation of the world's food and wine heritage. The philosophy is something we can all adopt in our lives: know the source of the ingredients you buy; make food from scratch; share and enjoy good food and wine with your family and friends.

swiss wedge Roesti

SERVES 2–3

300g (2 medium) old potatoes
2 tablespoons oil
butter
salt

Peel the potatoes, then immediately grate them coarsely by hand. Use your hands to wring out as much starch as possible.

Smear a shallow 18–20cm sloping-sided pan (use a cast iron, copper, heavy stainless steel or teflon-coated pan) with a little oil and set it over a medium-high heat. Allow the oil to get quite hot, but not smoking hot.

Drop in a knob of butter and swirl the pan until the butter melts and foams, then put in the grated potato. Spread it into a round shape, neatening the edges, then pat the surface lightly to knock out excess air.

Cook the roesti for about 5 minutes or until it is a good golden brown, shaking the pan from time to time to ensure it doesn't stick. Flip it over, or slide it onto a plate, cover with a second plate, invert it and slip it back into the pan. Drop in several small pieces of butter around the sides of the pan. As the butter melts, allow it to run under the roesti. Sprinkle with salt and cook for about 5 minutes or until golden brown on the bottom. Turn it out onto a heated serving plate, cut into wedges and serve immediately.

Roesti is a *Swiss potato cake. Use old potatoes, which are full of starch – new ones don't contain enough starch to hold them together. However, it's necessary to wring out excess starch and moisture, or the roesti will be gummy and won't become crisp. An all-purpose potato, such as a late season Desiree, is perfect.*

If you want to make roesti for more than two or three people, double the ingredients, but cook the mixture in two frying pans, or in two batches, rather than attempting to make one big roesti, which never works out well.

I personally love these roesti with little more than a decent tomato and a handful of rocket leaves – it balances the 'naughty factor' of the potatoes, butter, oil and salt quite well.

basque-ing Piperade

SERVES 6

2 tablespoons olive oil
1 large onion, finely sliced
4 cloves garlic, crushed
6 large peppers (capsicums), cored, deseeded and finely diced
1kg ripe outdoor tomatoes, skinned, cored and diced
scant $\frac{1}{2}$ teaspoon salt
freshly ground black pepper to taste
1 tablespoon finely chopped basil (optional)
4 eggs, at room temperature

Heat the oil in a large frying pan over a medium-low heat. Add the onion and fry gently until golden, stirring often. Add the garlic and cook a few more minutes, then add the prepared peppers. Cook for 15 minutes, stirring occasionally, then add the tomatoes. Cook for about 45 minutes, stirring often (especially towards the end of cooking), or until the mixture is thick and pulpy. Stir in the salt, black pepper and basil, if using.

If you are making the dish ahead of serving time (up to a day in advance is fine), add the salt and black pepper at this point, but add the basil when reheating as the flavour will be fresher. Cool, cover and refrigerate, then reheat in a clean frying pan when required.

Break the eggs into a bowl, beat with a fork, then pour into the pepper mixture. Cook gently, stirring, until the eggs are well combined and just cooked; the mixture should remain creamy and must not be overcooked. Serve immediately.

Think late summer: *sun-ripened tomatoes and peppers cooked to a pulp and bound together into a soft, creamy emulsion with fresh eggs – distinctly Basque!*

I like it equally with all red peppers, which are sweeter, or with 1–2 green peppers in place of some of the red, which introduces a touch of bitterness.

Serve with hot bread, brioche or croissants. Bacon and ham also make good partners.

top knot
Mushroom-filled Brioche

SERVES 6 OR MORE

9 small brioche (you may need to order these from a French bakery)
50g butter, melted, plus a little extra
6 spring onions, sliced
350g small button mushrooms, wiped clean with a cloth and sliced
$\frac{1}{4}$ cup dry white wine
$\frac{1}{4}$ teaspoon salt
freshly ground black pepper to taste
$1\frac{1}{2}$ tablespoons plain flour
$\frac{3}{4}$ cup water or light stock

Carefully slice off the 'top knots' on the brioche, using a small serrated knife (a grapefruit knife makes quick work of this), and carefully pick out some of the soft crumbs from the centre, forming a cavity for the filling. Brush inside and outside with the melted butter and put the brioche and the top knots in an ovenproof dish.

Melt a large knob of butter in a frying pan and add the spring onions. Cook very gently until wilted (don't let them brown). Transfer the spring onions to a plate. Increase the heat under the pan and add another large knob of butter.

When hot, add the mushrooms and toss quickly to coat in the butter. Cook over a medium heat, stirring often, until the mushrooms soften and give off liquid, then increase the heat to medium-high and cook until the liquid evaporates.

Pour in the wine, cook until it evaporates, then season with salt and black pepper. Sprinkle the flour over, stir it in and blend the water in. Bring to a gentle boil, turn to low and cook gently for 2–3 minutes, stirring. Cover with a lid and set aside.

About 20 minutes before serving, put the brioche in an oven preheated to 175°C and toast for 15 minutes or until crisp. Add the spring onions to the mushroom filling and reheat gently. Spoon the mushroom filling into the brioche and top with the lids. Serve immediately.

biting green Huevos con Chorizo

SERVES 2–4

400g (medium) waxy potatoes, peeled and finely diced

salt

1½ tablespoons butter

2 softish chorizo sausages, thinly sliced

4 free-range eggs

soft tortillas

4 tablespoons Mexican green chilli salsa, or to taste (or use a chilli salsa of your choice)

½ cup crumbled feta cheese (choose a firm, dryish type, not a squishy one)

2 tablespoons chopped coriander

The morning after a big night out, try this dish – it'll hit you 'thwack' between the ears and bring you back to life. Protein, carbohydrate, salt and fat never tasted so good – and to get rid of the cobwebs, splash on as much head-lifting chilli salsa as you dare.

Put the potatoes in a small saucepan, cover with cold water, salt lightly and bring to the boil. Lower the heat and cook, partially covered, until nearly tender. Drain, then tip onto a double thickness of absorbent kitchen paper.

Put the butter in a heavy-based or non-stick frying pan and set it over a medium heat. Add the potatoes and cook for about 15 minutes, turning often, or until crisp. Add the chorizo sausages and cook for 2–3 minutes, taking care not to let them burn.

Break the eggs into a bowl, add a good pinch of salt and beat with a fork.

Remove the pan from the heat and let it cool down. Pour in the eggs, set the pan back over a gentle heat and cook, stirring the egg from time to time with a wooden scraper, until it is nearly set but still creamy. Alternatively, cook the eggs in a small knob of butter in a clean pan.

Meanwhile, heat the tortillas one at a time in a dry non-stick frying pan until they are heated through. Put them on plates and distribute the egg and potato mixture over them.

Spoon over as much chilli salsa as you dare, then top with the crumbled feta cheese and coriander. Serve immediately.

Huevos con Chorizo

sultry

salty

light

alfresco

relax

summery

pleasure

sun-filled

water's

perfumed leisure

Mushroom Salad with Green Peppercorns

Spaghetti Luna Rossa

Zucchini, Peppers, Potatoes and Olives

Sweet Potato Salad

Butter Beans with Green Pepper and Tomatoes

Cos Salad with Warm Shallot Dressing

Fried Green Tomatoes

Sweet Corn, Tomato and Avocado Salad

Zucchini and Oregano Flan

Summer Vegetable Toss

Mediterranean Salad

Roasted Red Peppers with Creamy Fennel Sauce

Potato and Green Bean Salad with Cherry Tomatoes

Summer Salad

Sunburst Salad

Pawpaw and Avocado Salad with Ginger and Mint

Greek Tomatoes

Chick Pea and Coriander Salad

flavourful edge

champion Mushroom Salad with Green Peppercorns

SERVES 6–8

**500g fresh white button mushrooms, wiped with
   a damp cloth**
grated zest of 1 lemon
75ml lemon juice
75ml extra virgin olive oil
1 teaspoon salt
freshly ground black pepper to taste
1 rounded teaspoon drained green peppercorns
1 tablespoon coarsely chopped parsley
1 tablespoon finely chopped fresh thyme
**1 tablespoon finely chopped fresh marjoram
   or 1 tablespoon snipped chives**

Trim the mushroom stalks if necessary, then slice the mushrooms and put them in a bowl.

Whisk the lemon zest, lemon juice, oil, salt and black pepper together in a bowl. Blend in the green peppercorns and herbs, then pour the dressing over the mushrooms. Toss well and leave to marinate for 30 minutes, tossing occasionally. Before serving, toss well and transfer to a serving bowl.

Although the salad is at its best while the mushrooms are still slightly crunchy, it can be made up to 24 hours in advance. Cover, keep it chilled and serve cold.

If you are given the option of buying mushrooms in a plastic bag or a brown paper bag, always choose the latter. Mushrooms stored in plastic (at room temperature or in the fridge) quickly sweat and become soggy, then go rotten. Store them either in an unsealed brown paper bag or unsealed in a large plastic bag or container lined with absorbent kitchen paper.

If you want an attractive white mushroom salad, one with clear juices, not browny black, use lemon juice in the dressing instead of vinegar; lemon juice has the effect of keeping everything clear and white.

stellar Spaghetti Luna Rossa

SERVES 6

5 tablespoons extra virgin olive oil
2 large cloves garlic, crushed
1 tiny dried 'bird's eye' chilli, crushed, or to taste
2 x 400g cans Italian tomatoes, mashed
salt
freshly ground black pepper to taste
500g spaghetti
1½ cups small cherry tomatoes, halved
20 or so fresh basil leaves
2 handfuls of fresh rocket leaves, trimmed
piece of fresh Italian parmesan cheese in the block

Put the oil in a saucepan. Heat gently and add the garlic and chilli. Cook until the garlic is just starting to colour, then pour in the tomatoes. Season with a little salt and black pepper and bring the sauce to the boil. Cook gently for about 30 minutes or until pulpy, stirring occasionally. The sauce can be made ahead and gently reheated when required.

Cook the spaghetti in plenty of boiling salted water until al dente. Take the sauce off the heat and add the cherry tomatoes and basil to the hot sauce. Drain the spaghetti and turn it into a bowl. Toss the sauce through, then strew the top with rocket leaves. Toss again, then scatter the parmesan over. Serve immediately.

My sister-in-law, *Isanna, made this dish for me when she stayed with me. She called it Bell'Italia but, during the nail-biting 2000 Louis Vuitton Cup boat races in Auckland between Italy's Prada and America One, I felt urged to rename it in Prada's honour because we ate the dish so often that summer; Luna Rossa was the name of their boat.*

It's a fabulous pasta dish – unique because although it is basically a tomato sauce with spaghetti, adding whole cherry tomatoes, rocket leaves and parmesan lifts it into the special category. The cherry tomatoes don't cook in the sauce, they stay intact and provide juicy bursts of sweet tomato flavour. The rocket adds pepperiness. It's just gorgeous!

texture Zucchini, Peppers, Potatoes and Olives

SERVES 4

600g waxy or salad potatoes, peeled and cut into quarters and shaped into ovals with a potato peeler
salt
3 zucchini (courgettes), cut in half lengthways, then into chunks and shaped into ovals with a potato peeler
2 large red peppers (capsicums), cored, deseeded and cut into thickish strips
3 tablespoons extra virgin olive oil
1 large clove garlic, crushed
freshly ground black pepper to taste
12 Kalamata olives

Steam or gently boil the potatoes until just tender (salt them lightly). Blanch the zucchini in boiling salted water for 1 minute, drain and refresh with plenty of cold water. Dry on absorbent kitchen paper. Put the red peppers and olive oil in a large frying pan over a high heat. Cook for 3 minutes, stirring, then add the garlic, ¼ teaspoon of salt and black pepper. Lower the heat and cook gently for 5 minutes. The dish can be prepared ahead to this point.

If prepared ahead, reheat the peppers. Add the potatoes, zucchini and olives to the pan and cook gently, stirring occasionally, until piping hot. Transfer to a heated bowl and serve immediately.

This dish *is colourful and has a good contrast of textures. It's imperative to use waxy potatoes; starchy ones will collapse. If you can't be bothered with the fiddle of shaping the vegetables, don't – just cut them into chunks. Fresh baby zucchini are a wonderful vegetable, quite different from the large watery ones sometimes sold. They can be eaten raw, sliced thinly, dressed with a vinaigrette and served as a salad. Raw zucchini also make good containers for savoury bits and bobs – halve them, scoop out the centre (chop and add it to the filling), then fill with the chosen stuffing and bake.*

creamy Sweet Potato Salad

SERVES 6

700g sweet potatoes, peeled and cut into large chunks
salt
125g streaky bacon
2 oranges
2 tablespoons plump raisins
freshly ground black pepper to taste
$\frac{1}{4}$ cup mayonnaise

Put the sweet potato chunks in a metal colander or steaming basket over a saucepan of boiling water. Sprinkle a little salt over, cover with a lid or aluminium foil and steam for 12–15 minutes or until just tender. Remove the colander or steaming basket from the saucepan and allow the sweet potatoes to cool quickly. Cut into large cubes.

Fry the bacon rashers until crisp in a large heated non-stick frying pan, or fry (or grill) it in your normal way. Tilt the pan to drain away any fat, transfer the bacon to a board and chop coarsely. Set aside.

Fillet the oranges as described below. Squeeze all the juice from the membrane into the bowl, then add the sweet potatoes and raisins. Sprinkle with a little salt and grind on some black pepper. Toss well, then stir in the mayonnaise. Transfer to a serving bowl and scatter the bacon over the top.

The salad keeps well, covered and refrigerated, for 1–2 days. The addition of 1–2 stalks of stringed celery (run a vegetable peeler lengthways down each stalk), finely sliced, adds a bit more crunch.

Filleting oranges
Using a gentle sawing movement, remove the peel from the oranges with a small serrated knife, taking off all the white pith. Make a cut on both sides of each piece of membrane and the segments will come away easily; drop them into a bowl.

imbued Butter Beans with Green Pepper and Tomatoes

SERVES 4

3 tablespoons extra virgin olive oil
1 medium onion, finely sliced
1 large clove garlic, crushed
1 large green pepper (capsicum)
$\frac{1}{2}$ cup mashed Italian canned tomatoes
$\frac{1}{2}$ teaspoon salt
freshly ground black pepper to taste
500g butter beans, topped and tailed
$\frac{1}{4}$ cup water

Heat the oil in a heavy-based saucepan and add the onion and garlic. Cover with a lid and cook very gently for about 10 minutes or until softish.

If the green pepper is fleshy, peel off the outside skin with a vegetable peeler (the skin of fleshy peppers tends to separate from the flesh during cooking), then remove the core and seeds. Slice the flesh thinly and add it to the pan along with the tomatoes, salt and black pepper.

Cover and cook gently for about 12 minutes or until the mixture thickens like a sauce; be careful not to let it catch on the bottom of the pan. Tip in the butter beans, toss them to coat with the mixture, then add the water.

Cover the pan and cook gently for about 15 minutes. If there is not much liquid left after this time, and the beans are not tender, add a little more water. Continue cooking until the beans are very tender. Serve hot.

A red pepper can be used instead of a green one, but I like the hint of bitterness provided by a green pepper set against the sweeter flavours of the onion and tomato.

The butter beans can be cooked ahead of time, cooled, then reheated carefully.

my way   Cos Salad with Warm Shallot Dressing

SERVES 4

3 slices day-old toast bread
olive oil for cooking croûtons
Maldon sea salt
1 large cos lettuce, broken apart, washed and dried
small block Italian parmesan cheese
4 very fresh free-range eggs
4 tablespoons extra virgin olive oil
1 large clove garlic, crushed
3 shallots (eschallots), finely sliced
2 good tomatoes, skinned, deseeded and diced
1½ tablespoons white wine vinegar
freshly ground black pepper to taste
2 tablespoons chopped chervil (optional)

Remove the crusts from the bread and cut it into small squares. Heat $\frac{1}{3}$ cup of oil in a frying pan over a medium heat and, when it is hot but just before it starts hazing, drop in the bread cubes. Cook quickly, tossing them until they are well browned. Tilt the pan then, using a slotted spoon, transfer the croûtons to a plate lined with absorbent kitchen paper. Sprinkle the croûtons with salt, then set aside.

Arrange the cos lettuce in four pasta or soup bowls. Cut the parmesan into slivers with a vegetable peeler and distribute amongst the bowls along with the croûtons.

Poach the eggs as described in the recipe for Spinach Florentine (see page 40).

While the eggs are poaching, set a pan over a medium-low heat and add the oil, garlic and shallots. Let the shallots cook gently for a few minutes (don't let the pan get too hot – they mustn't fry), then tip the tomatoes and vinegar in with a sprinkling of salt and black pepper. Cook for 1–2 minutes more, then add the chervil, if using. Put the drained eggs in the salad bowls, pour the dressing over and serve immediately.

The trouble with being a perceived 'foodie' is that people expect you to eat everything. Well, I don't! I'm a confessed anchovy hater and consequently I rarely order a Caesar salad when I'm in a restaurant because it feels picky saying 'hold the anchovies'. I'm fighting back though. This is Caesar salad my way, with not an anchovy in sight – and it is very good! Try it for a spring lunch.

hot damn Fried Green Tomatoes

SERVES 8

8 large unripe green outdoor tomatoes
salt
extra virgin olive oil
$\frac{1}{2}$ cup plain flour

Wash and dry the tomatoes. Cut them into slices 1.5cm thick and sprinkle on both sides with salt. Arrange them on a wire cake rack and leave to drain for 1 hour, then turn them and drain for a further hour. Just prior to cooking, pat them very dry with absorbent kitchen paper. Put the flour on a piece of absorbent kitchen paper.

Pour a 1cm depth of oil into a large heavy-based frying pan. Heat the oil over a high heat. When it is shimmering and starting to haze, quickly coat about half the tomatoes with flour then lower them into the oil. Cook until golden on both sides, then remove them with a slotted spatula, transferring them to a serving plate. Sprinkle with salt and serve hot. Allow the oil to get hot again, then continue cooking the rest of the tomatoes.

The sharp bite *of green tomatoes is enhanced by the fruitiness of the extra virgin olive oil. The dish calls for an accompaniment of good bread, perhaps a fennel-seed flavoured sausage or two and a steaming mound of fluffy whipped potato. Ecstasy comes cheap on a summer's eve! Just remember to start the tomatoes about 2 hours before you need to cook them. Obviously, it's important to use outdoor tomatoes of good heritage to ensure the correct texture.*

And one more point — don't skimp on the oil. If it is not deep enough, the temperature of it will be lowered dramatically when the tomatoes go in and they will collapse and become soggy instead of crisp and browned. Don't fret about wasting oil. Olive oil, unlike many other oils, can be reused dozens of times — let it cool and settle, then strain it into a bottle, cover and keep it in a cool dark place until required.

silk Sweet Corn, Tomato and Avocado Salad

SERVES 6–8

6 ears fresh sweet corn, husks and silk removed
2 large red outdoor tomatoes
3 tablespoons extra virgin olive oil
1 tablespoon lemon juice
$\frac{1}{2}$ teaspoon Dijon mustard
$\frac{1}{2}$ teaspoon salt
freshly ground black pepper to taste
1 tablespoon finely chopped shallot (eschallot)
2 tablespoons torn basil leaves
1 ripe but firm avocado, peeled and stone removed

Cook the sweet corn in plenty of boiling water for 10–20 minutes (allow 10 minutes or less for fresh-picked cobs and 20 minutes for cobs that were picked 1–2 days ago). Drain and drape with a piece of absorbent kitchen paper (this keeps in steam and keeps the kernels moist and plump — they dry and turn wrinkly otherwise). When the corn is cool enough to handle, slice off the kernels and transfer them to a platter.

Cut the tomatoes into quarters, cutting out the cores, and flick out as many seeds as possible. Cut the flesh into dice, put in a sieve and leave to drain for 10 minutes.

Mix the oil, lemon juice, mustard, salt, black pepper, shallot and basil together in a bowl. Top the sweet corn with the drained tomatoes and diced avocado, whisk the dressing and and pour it on. Give a gentle stir to amalgamate, then serve immediately.

tart Zucchini and Oregano Flan

SERVES 4–6

25cm flan ring lined with rich shortcrust pastry, chilled (see opposite)
700g (7–8) small yellow or green zucchini (courgettes), trimmed
knob of butter
1 small onion, finely chopped
$\frac{1}{2}$ teaspoon salt
freshly ground black pepper to taste
2 eggs and 1 egg yolk
200ml cream
$\frac{1}{4}$ teaspoon dried oregano
$\frac{1}{2}$ cup freshly grated Italian parmesan cheese

Line the pastry with a double thickness of crumpled tissue paper and fill with baking beans or rice. Bake the pastry for 15 minutes in an oven preheated to 180°C. Remove from the oven and lift off the paper and beans or rice. (The beans or rice can be cooled, then kept in a container for future 'blind baking'.) Prick the pastry base with a fork then return it to the oven for 10–12 minutes or until lightly browned all over. Remove from the oven.

Meanwhile, slice half of the zucchini very thinly on the diagonal and set aside for the top. Slice the rest of the zucchini into thinnish rounds and put them in a large frying pan with the butter and onion. Sprinkle with salt and grind on some black pepper, then cook gently until softened but not browned (about 10 minutes). Cool.

Beat the eggs and egg yolk together with the cream and add the oregano. Tip the cooked zucchini into the pastry case, level the top and arrange the raw zucchini on the top in concentric rings. Spoon the egg mixture over, ensuring all the top slices of zucchini are coated, then sprinkle the parmesan on top. (There is a generous amount of cheese. Use it all because it not only flavours the tart but also helps it colour.)

Bake the tart for 15 minutes or until golden on top. Serve warm, cut into slices.

Rich Shortcrust Pastry

225g plain flour
pinch of salt
170g butter, softened and pliable but not oily
1 egg yolk
3–4 tablespoons ice-cold water (chill the water in the freezer)

Sift the flour and salt into a large mixing bowl. Cut the butter into large lumps and drop it into the flour. Using two knives, cut the butter through the flour until the pieces of butter are like small marbles. Use your fingertips to rub the butter into the flour until the mixture resembles coarse breadcrumbs.

Mix the egg yolk and water together and add it all at once to the flour mixture (use 3 tablespoons of water to begin with; if the pastry seems a little dry and flaky during mixing, sprinkle the remaining water onto the dry flakes). Stir with a knife to combine. Lightly knead with the hands and turn out onto a cool, dry, lightly floured surface. Knead briefly until smooth. Wrap in plastic food wrap and refrigerate for 30 minutes (this is important, as it allows the fat to cool and firm, which will prevent sticking during rolling out, and it relaxes the gluten in the flour, which will help minimise shrinkage).

Roll out thinly, using a smooth rolling pin, with short rolls, rolling away from your body. Occasionally flour the rolling pin and the board underneath the pastry to prevent sticking. Don't flour the top of the pastry, as the flour will get rolled in and can make the surface of the pastry dry. Cut and shape as required.

tangle Summer Vegetable Toss

SERVES 6

4 ears fresh sweet corn
700g (7–8) small firm zucchini (courgettes), trimmed
$2\frac{1}{2}$ tablespoons extra virgin olive oil
handful of small basil leaves
1 large red onion, sliced
1 red pepper (capsicum), cored, deseeded and
**   sliced**
$\frac{1}{2}$ teaspoon salt
freshly ground black pepper to taste

Remove the husks and silk from the sweet corn, then boil the cobs gently for 10–20 minutes (allow 10 minutes or less for fresh-picked cobs and 20 minutes for cobs that were picked 1–2 days ago). Drain and drape with a piece of absorbent kitchen paper until cool enough to handle (this keeps in steam and keeps the kernels moist and plump – they dry and turn wrinkly otherwise).

Slice the zucchini into long thin strips with a potato peeler. Heat 2 tablespoons of the oil in a large heavy-based frying pan over a medium heat. When hot, drop in the zucchini slices and cook for a few minutes until wilting (don't overcook), tossing gently with tongs. Transfer to a large serving bowl and scatter half the basil over. Put the rest of the oil in the pan, lower the heat and add the onion and red pepper. Cook gently for about 5–10 minutes until the onion is nearly tender. Add to the zucchini, sprinkle with salt and grind on some black pepper.

Cut the kernels off the sweet corn cobs with a large sharp knife and add to the bowl of vegetables. If you want to keep the corn in long strips of kernels, cook it ahead and cool it before slicing it off the cob; if you slice sweet corn while it is hot, it separates into kernels. Mix gently together, scatter the rest of the basil over and serve hot or warmish.

Along with green beans, *corn and zucchini (or other members of the squash family) form the trinity known as 'The Three Sisters' in southern American gardening lore. When beans and corn are grown together, the beans draw nitrogen from the soil, which the corn thrives on. Squash and pumpkin, with their prickly vines, are planted around the beans and corn to stop pesky wild animals destroying the plants. It's a combination you might like to try in your own garden.*

Traditional advice, to put the water on to boil before going down to the corn patch to pick the corn, has plenty of merit. As soon as the sweet corn is cut from the plant, the sugar starts turning to starch, so the sooner you get it in the pot, the sweeter it's going to be. New varieties of corn retain the sugar longer before it converts to starch, but speed is still essential; no amount of care and gentle massaging is going to resurrect withered corn cobs. Another adage that is also true is don't salt the water until the corn is cooked; salt it at the table, because if added during cooking, salt toughens the kernels.

If you want to check the degree of ripeness on growing corn, open a cob and prick the kernels. If the juice is clear, the cob is not yet ready to pick. If the juice is milky, don't hesitate – go back and put the water on to boil. If there is no liquid, the corn is past its best. Once picked, put the corn in its husks in a plastic bag and refrigerate it. Remove the husks just prior to cooking.

Corn is a high carbohydrate food, with good quantities of Vitamin A and B, and some C. It contains potassium, moderate amounts of protein and hardly any fat.

Summer Vegetable Toss

snappy Mediterranean Salad

SERVES 4–6

300g slim green beans, topped and tailed
salt
1 large red pepper (capsicum), roasted (see page 20)
freshly ground black pepper to taste
2 tablespoons extra virgin olive oil
1 clove garlic, crushed
1 tablespoon snipped chives
1 tablespoon chopped basil
$\frac{1}{2}$ teaspoon finely chopped rosemary
250g feta marinated in olive oil, or similar firm white cheese, drained and sliced thinly

Plunge the beans into a saucepan of boiling salted water and cook until just tender. Drain and refresh with cold water until the beans feel cool. Dry off on absorbent kitchen paper.

Peel the skin off the roasted pepper, remove the core and seeds and cut into dice, reserving any juices.

When ready to assemble the salad, put 2 tablespoons of pepper juices in a bowl, add $\frac{1}{4}$ teaspoon of salt, black pepper, the olive oil, garlic and herbs. Blend well.

Arrange the beans, cheese and red pepper on a serving plate or in a bowl, spoon the dressing over and serve.

This works as *a starter for six people, served with hot garlicky bread and a glass of chilled rosé wine, or it can be part of an all-vegetable meal, providing protein as well as vibrant colour and interesting texture. Just a word about the rosemary: a scant $\frac{1}{2}$ teaspoon, finely chopped, is all you need – any more and it will overpower everything.*

The best *beans in the world, in my opinion, are the scarlet runners I grow in my garden every summer. They're unbelievably crisp and juicy and full of flavour, and my daughter, Ilaria, and I often stand in the bean patch in summer scoffing them raw. My dad's a bean fanatic too – he's made many a meal of a steaming plate of beans well seasoned with a lump of fresh butter and plenty of salt and black pepper, accompanied by a handle of chilled beer and a door-stopper slice of white bread. At nearly 90 he's still going strong.*

So what's so good about garden-fresh beans? The snap, the juice, the sweet flavour, which you'll never get from a bean that has been picked, packed, transported, presented and purchased.

charred Roasted Red Peppers with Creamy Fennel Sauce

SERVES 8–10

11 red peppers (capsicums)
extra virgin olive oil
10 cloves garlic, peeled and sliced
freshly ground black pepper to taste
3 tablespoons water
125ml cream
pinch of salt
pinch of castor sugar
$1\frac{1}{2}$ teaspoons fennel seeds

Cut the peppers in half and deseed them but leave the cores intact. Rub the peppers lightly with olive oil and put them on two baking trays. Distribute the garlic amongst them and grind on some black pepper. Cook for 20–30 minutes or until charred, in an oven preheated to 200°C.

When the peppers are cool, use a teaspoon to scrape the juices and garlic from them into the bowl of a food processor. Peel 1 pepper (2 halves), chop coarsely, and add to the processor bowl with the water. Blend until smooth. Put the remaining peppers in an ovenproof serving dish.

The peppers can be prepared several hours ahead to this point; reheat them briefly in a hot oven just before serving.

Put the cream in a small frying pan with the puréed pepper mixture and add the salt, a little freshly ground black pepper, the sugar and fennel seeds. Reduce by one-third over a medium-high heat. Pour into the peppers and serve hottish.

This is an *excellent vegetarian dish, which, because of the cream, provides richness to a meal. The peppers go fabulously with rice – I've successfully teamed them with a vegetable paella but any rice dish will do. The fennel seeds are sneaky things – they stop the creamy filling from making the peppers too rich and help aid digestion.*

Roasted Red Peppers with Creamy Fennel Sauce

warm Potato and Green Bean Salad with Cherry Tomatoes

SERVES 4

400g waxy potatoes
salt
200g slim green beans, topped and tailed
1 large clove garlic, crushed
¼ teaspoon Dijon mustard
freshly ground black pepper to taste
1 tablespoon white wine vinegar or tarragon
  vinegar
4 tablespoons extra virgin olive oil
1 cup yellow cherry tomatoes
½ cup red cherry tomatoes (or use all red tomatoes
  if yellow are not available)
½ cup small basil leaves (optional)
4 cups picked-over salad leaves (watercress, corn
  salad, endive)

Peel the potatoes. Unless the potatoes are very small, cut them into chunks. Put them in a saucepan, cover with cold water, salt lightly and bring to the boil. Cook gently until nearly tender, then drain and leave to cool (they will finish cooking in their own steam).

Plunge the beans into a saucepan of boiling salted water and cook for 3–4 minutes or until crisp-tender. Drain and refresh with cold water, then dry with absorbent kitchen paper.

In a large bowl mix the garlic, mustard, black pepper, vinegar and ¼ teaspoon of salt together, then whisk in the oil; this can be prepared ahead.

Add the warm potatoes, warm beans and cherry tomatoes to the dressing and toss gently. Scatter the basil over, if using, and add the salad leaves. Toss again, then serve immediately.

ripe Summer Salad

SERVES 4

3 ears fresh sweet corn, husks and silk removed
2 tablespoons lemon juice
½ teaspoon salt
good grinding of black pepper
1 clove garlic, crushed
5 tablespoons extra virgin olive oil
1 red pepper and 1 yellow pepper (capsicum),
  halved, cored and cut into thin strips
½ cup black olives, stoned
1 tablespoon chopped parsley
1 tablespoon snipped chives
1 tablespoon chopped basil
1 ripe but firm avocado

Cook the sweet corn in plenty of boiling water for 10–20 minutes (allow 10 minutes or less for fresh-picked cobs and 20 minutes for cobs that were picked 1–2 days ago). Drain and drape with a piece of absorbent kitchen paper (this keeps in steam and keeps the kernels moist and plump – they dry and turn wrinkly otherwise). When the corn is cool enough to handle, slice off the kernels and transfer to a platter.

Whisk the lemon juice, salt, black pepper and garlic together in a small bowl, then blend the oil in. Put the sweet corn, peppers, olives, parsley, chives and basil in a large bowl and toss lightly with the dressing.

Peel the avocado and cut into cubes. Add to the salad, toss lightly, then serve.

Potato and Green Bean Salad with Cherry Tomatoes

golden yolks
Sunburst Salad

SERVES 4

6 peppers (capsicums) of assorted hues
2 free-range eggs, at room temperature
juice of $\frac{1}{2}$ lemon
zest of $\frac{1}{2}$ orange
1 tablespoon snipped chives
$\frac{1}{4}$ teaspoon salt
freshly ground black pepper to taste
1 tablespoon capers, drained
4 tablespoons walnut oil
several black olives
sweet ground paprika

Put the peppers on an oven rack in an oven preheated to 200°C and cook for about 20 minutes, turning occasionally with tongs, or until they are blistered and charred. Transfer them to a board and allow to cool. Peel off the skins and slip out and discard the cores and seeds. Slice the peppers into strips and arrange on a large plate.

Hard-boil the eggs by lowering them into a saucepan of gently boiling water. Cook gently for 7 minutes, shell them and cut into quarters (see below). Arrange in the centre of the peppers.

In a small bowl whisk the lemon juice, orange zest, chives (reserve a few for garnishing), salt, black pepper and capers, then whisk in the walnut oil. Spoon over the peppers and eggs. Decorate with the olives and reserved snipped chives, then sieve a little paprika over. Serve immediately with crusty bread.

'Hard-boiled eggs' *is a misnomer. If you literally boil eggs until hard, the whites will have turned tough and rubbery and the yolks will be solid, and they will be difficult to digest. I prefer to add the eggs to boiling water, rather than starting them in cold water and bringing them to the boil, because it is easier to judge the cooking time accurately. They should be cooked in gently boiling water.*

When you first lower the eggs into the water, carefully roll them around the pot for a few seconds. This sets the yolks in the centre.

To prevent the shells from cracking during cooking, use the point of a dressmaking pin to prick the rounded end of each egg, where there is a small air-sac. The pin hole acts like an escape valve; as the contents of the egg swell during cooking, they force the air out of the air-sac, preventing the shell from cracking.

Having the eggs at room temperature and bringing them slowly to the boil also helps.

It is just about impossible to shell very fresh eggs which have been hard-boiled; use eggs that are several days old (use fresh ones for poaching or frying).

Once the eggs have had their cooking time, pour off the boiling water and run cold tap water over them for a few minutes to cool them quickly; this stops a grey sulphur ring forming around the yolk.

squeeze Pawpaw and Avocado Salad with Ginger and Mint

SERVES 6

1 large or 2 small pawpaw, ripe but firm
2 ripe but firm avocados
1 lemon plus $\frac{1}{4}$ cup lemon juice
small knob fresh ginger
$\frac{1}{2}$ cup canola oil
salt
1 fresh hot red chilli, halved, deseeded and very finely chopped
2 tablespoons mint, chopped

Peel the pawpaw, cut in half and scoop out the seeds. Cut the flesh into cubes.

Cut the avocados in half, extract the stones, remove skins and slice or cut into cubes. Arrange the pawpaw and avocados on a platter. Sprinkle with a little lemon juice.

Peel and grate the ginger coarsely, then squeeze with the fingers to extract the juice, letting the juice fall into a bowl. Mix with the oil, a few pinches of salt, and the $\frac{1}{4}$ cup of lemon juice. Spoon over the salad. Scatter the chopped chilli and mint over. Serve immediately.

An unlikely combination, *perhaps, but this dish is memorable not only for the colours, fragrance and hot chilli zing set against fresh mint and lemon, but because it is the quintessential summer salad to serve with a side of moist freshly smoked fish. There's enough dressing to saturate everything, and enough to sog crunchy bread. Scrumptious!*

Pawpaw and Avocado Salad with Ginger and Mint

pulp Greek Tomatoes

SERVES 6–12

12 large outdoor tomatoes
salt
1 tablespoon castor sugar
freshly ground black pepper to taste
$\frac{1}{2}$ cup olive oil
1 large onion, finely chopped
1 cup short or medium grain rice, washed and
    drained
2 tablespoons pine nuts (optional)
$\frac{1}{2}$ cup currants
1 tablespoon finely chopped mint
1 tablespoon finely chopped parsley
1 cup water
1 tablespoon dried breadcrumbs
extra virgin olive oil for drizzling

Wash the tomatoes and cut a thin slice off each from the 'flower' end (not the end with the stalk). Set these slices aside to use as caps. Use a small teaspoon to scoop out the tomato pulp, transferring it to a sieve set over a bowl, then sprinkle the inside of each tomato with salt and castor sugar and grind on a little black pepper. Put the tomatoes in an oiled baking dish, preferably one in which they fit snugly. Leave the tomato pulp to drain for 5 minutes, then discard the accumulated liquid. Pass the pulp through the sieve and set aside.

Heat the oil in a large frying pan and cook the onion until soft and transparent, then tip in the rice and fry for 1–2 minutes. Add the pine nuts, if using, the currants, mint, parsley, $\frac{1}{2}$ teaspoon of salt and black pepper. Stir well, then blend in $\frac{1}{2}$ cup of the tomato pulp and the water.

Cover and cook very gently for 10 minutes or until the rice is half cooked. Spoon the mixture into the prepared tomatoes (don't over-fill them) and top with the reserved slices of tomato. Sprinkle the breadcrumbs over then drizzle with a little extra virgin olive oil. Pour in $\frac{1}{2}$ cup of tomato pulp, then bake for about 30 minutes in an oven preheated to 180°C. If the tomato pulp dries up during cooking, add a little more. Serve warm or at room temperature.

The tomatoes for this dish must be ripe but firm, red and flavoursome, bursting with summer sun. This is the sort of dish which is served in large buckled black trays in tavernas all through Greece. Team it up with a loaf of good bread, a salad of baby green leaves including a handful of bitter or peppery leaves, a hunk of feta and a bowl of olives.

quick Chick Pea and Coriander Salad

SERVES 6

50ml extra virgin olive oil
$1\frac{1}{2}$ tablespoons lemon juice
$\frac{1}{4}$ teaspoon salt, or more to taste
freshly ground black pepper to taste
1 large clove garlic, crushed
2 x 300g cans chick peas, drained, rinsed and
    drained again (or use 2 cups cooked chick peas)
1 yellow or red pepper (capsicum), cored,
    deseeded and sliced thinly into short lengths
2 tablespoons finely chopped coriander

Whisk the oil, lemon juice, salt, black pepper and garlic together in a bowl. Add the chick peas, sliced pepper and coriander. Toss well and serve. The salad keeps well, covered and refrigerated, for up to 24 hours.

aglow

heat-freak

fire

hothead

melt

ignite

dragon's

fiery

chilli-load

excite

stimulate

Spicy Fried Potatoes

Cashew Nut Curry

South of the Border Soup

Sambar

Curried Cauliflower and Potato

Stirfry Spinach and Eggplant

Indian Peas, Spuds and Mushrooms

Bharat's Dhal

Gujarati Eggplant and Potato Curry

Spicy Pumpkin

breath

inferno

sizzle Spicy Fried Potatoes

SERVES 4

50g butter

**1kg waxy potatoes, peeled, cut into large cubes
and dried with absorbent kitchen paper**

4 cloves garlic, crushed

1 teaspoon chilli powder

1 teaspoon ground cumin

1 teaspoon turmeric

1 teaspoon salt

freshly ground black pepper to taste

**1 large red pepper (capsicum), cored, deseeded
and diced**

2 tomatoes, skinned, cored, deseeded and diced

$\frac{3}{4}$ cup water

$\frac{1}{4}$ cup plain yoghurt, or more to taste

1 tablespoon finely chopped mint

Heat a large frying pan over a medium heat and drop in the butter. Allow it to melt, then add the potatoes. Toss well in the butter and fry until crisp and golden (takes about 40 minutes), turning often.

Add the garlic, spices, salt, black pepper and red pepper and cook for 5 minutes, stirring. Blend the tomatoes in, cook for 1 minute, then pour the water in. Cover with a lid and cook gently for 12–15 minutes or until the potatoes are tender.

Meanwhile, mix the yoghurt and mint together. Transfer the potatoes to a serving dish and drizzle the minty yoghurt over. Serve hot or at room temperature.

bathe Cashew Nut Curry

SERVES 6

2 cups desiccated coconut

2$\frac{1}{2}$ cups hot water

1$\frac{1}{2}$ tablespoons grated ginger

2 cloves garlic, crushed

1 medium onion, sliced

**2 fresh medium-hot red chillies, halved, deseeded
and each cut in half again**

**2 short lengths lemon grass, smashed with a
mallet, or 5–6 strips lemon peel**

small piece cinnamon bark

$\frac{1}{2}$ teaspoon ground turmeric

1 small stem curry leaves (optional)

$\frac{1}{2}$ teaspoon salt

250g raw cashew nuts

Put the desiccated coconut in a blender or food processor and pour in the hot water. Blend for 30 seconds, then tip into a sieve set over a bowl. Squeeze with your hands to extract the milk (alternatively, use ready-prepared coconut milk).

Measure 600ml of coconut milk and put in a saucepan with the ginger, garlic, onion, chillies, lemon grass or lemon rind, cinnamon bark, turmeric and curry leaves, if using.

Bring to a gentle boil, then cook, uncovered, for 12 minutes. Add the salt and cashew nuts, stir, then cook gently for 30 minutes or until the nuts are tender and the liquid is reduced. Transfer to a bowl and serve hottish.

This curry *of tender cashew nuts bathed in a rich coconutty sauce is utterly delicious! Don't be tempted to increase the chilli heat – the delicate spicing allows the cashews to be the star. The dish is easily doubled and it can be made up to a day in advance if required.*

mexican wave

South of the Border Soup

SERVES 6–8

1 teaspoon olive oil
½ teaspoon cumin seeds
1 fresh hot red chilli, halved, deseeded and roughly chopped
2 whole cloves
small stick cinnamon
750g plum tomatoes, peeled, deseeded and finely diced
1 small red onion, very finely chopped
1.5 litres fish stock (recipe follows)
1 small red pepper (capsicum), halved, deseeded and finely diced
2 limes, sliced into rounds
1½ teaspoons salt
700g–1kg skinned white fish fillets, rinsed
1 large ripe but firm avocado, peeled, stone removed, and diced
2 tablespoons roughly chopped coriander

Heat the oil in a small frying pan and add the cumin seeds, chilli, cloves and cinnamon. Cook briefly until the cumin seeds darken slightly, then turn off the heat, tilt the pan and leave to drain for a minute. Transfer the spice mixture to a blender and grind with 1 tablespoon of diced tomatoes.

Add the onion to the oil in the pan, along with 1 tablespoon of stock, and cook gently until transparent. Add the red pepper and cook for 2–3 minutes, adding a little more stock if the vegetables start to catch.

Blend in the tomatoes and cook for 10 minutes, stirring often, then transfer to a clean saucepan. Add the stock, spices, sliced limes and salt. Stir well, then add the fish. Cook very gently for about 5 minutes or until the fish is just cooked. Dish the soup, with whole pieces of fish, into hot soup bowls, garnish with avocado and coriander and serve.

Fish Stock

1 large fish frame, rinsed and broken into 2 pieces
1 carrot, cut into sticks
1 stalk celery, cut into sticks
1 leek, trimmed, well washed, cut into short lengths then quartered
peeled rind of 1 lime
1 teaspoon peppercorns
1 teaspoon coriander seeds
2 litres water

Put all the ingredients in a saucepan and bring to the boil. Lower the heat, then simmer gently for 20 minutes. Immediately strain into a bowl. Cool, then refrigerate. Use within 48 hours, or freeze for up to a month.

The pungency of coriander, *floral notes of lime, bursts of chilli and spice, capped with pale green cubes of velvety-textured avocado makes this soup the most intriguing I've ever eaten.*

If plum tomatoes are not available, substitute 2 x 400g cans Italian tomatoes, mashed.

Fish stock *is quick and easy to make and adds a flavour boost to soups, sauces and risottos made with seafood. Order a fish frame from the fishmonger (most are thrown away). Rinse it well, then cook it for 20 minutes only and strain it immediately. Prolonged cooking can make the stock too strong and gelatinous. If it is not drained quickly, but is left sitting around cooling with the fish frame still in it, it can develop a bitter taste. Fish stock can be frozen, but it is delicate in flavour and is best used within a month. To concentrate flavour, boil until well reduced.*

roll a roti Sambar

SERVES 6

½ cup red lentils
salt
½ teaspoon ground turmeric
50g tamarind pulp
1 small carrot, diced
1 small tomato, skinned and chopped
1 small zucchini (courgette), diced (or use a small amount of diced eggplant [aubergine])
3 teaspoons sambar powder (available at Indian spice shops)
1 teaspoon chilli powder
1½ tablespoons canola oil
½ teaspoon each mustard seeds, fenugreek and cumin seeds
½ teaspoon asafoetida powder
a few curry leaves
small bunch of coriander leaves

Wash the red lentils under running cold water until the water runs clear. Put them in a saucepan with 2½ cups of water, ¼ teaspoon of salt and the turmeric. Bring to the boil, then lower the heat and simmer gently, partially covered with a lid, for 30 minutes or until soft.

Put the tamarind pulp in a bowl with 1½ cups of hot water. When the water is cool, loosen the seeds and pulp from the pods, then sieve the mixture (see following).

Add the prepared vegetables to the lentils along with the sambar powder, chilli powder and the sieved tamarind pulp. Cook for about 30 minutes or until the vegetables are tender.

Heat the oil in a saucepan and add the mustard, fenugreek and cumin seeds and the asafoetida powder. When the mustards seeds start popping, lower the heat and pour the vegetable dhal mixture into the saucepan (take care doing this because it can splatter). Cook gently for 2–3 minutes, stirring. Add the curry leaves, transfer to a bowl and garnish with coriander.

This South Indian lentil dish has a delicious tang from tamarind and a fair bit of heat from chilli powder. It's good with roti and mixed curries.

Tamarind pulp is obtained from the pods of the tamarind tree and is used as a sour flavour in curries. It is sold in a slab with seeds and fibre. Break off a lump of tamarind and soak it in hot water. When the water is cool, break the tamarind apart with the fingers, massage the stones to release the pulp, then pass the pulp through a sieve to catch the seeds and fibre. Store unused tamarind, well wrapped, in the door of the refrigerator; it keeps well.

Sambar powder is a blend of spices and lentils used to flavour a dish of dhal which is given the same name. The powder is a rusty gold colour and smells of roasted spices and earthy lentils. It is warming in the mouth, not hot, with a mild acid finish.

For information on asafoetida, see page 80.

Spice seeds are usually briefly fried in oil to release their potent flavours. Ground spices burn easily and are usually cooked very quickly, or mixed into pastes or used raw. Mustard seeds pop and start jumping out of the pan when they are ready. Use a 'splatter screen' (a flat circular piece of wire mesh with a handle) to contain them.

Buy spices in small quantities and store them airtight. They quickly lose their fragrance and taste. If you don't believe me, drag out that jar of ground ginger from the back of your pantry and sniff it alongside some freshly purchased ginger – chalk and cheese!

smoking Curried Cauliflower and Potato

SERVES 8

50g butter
500g (3 large) waxy potatoes, peeled and cubed
½ cup vegetable oil
1 teaspoon black mustard seeds
1 onion, finely chopped
1 teaspoon lemon juice
1 teaspoon ground coriander seeds
1 teaspoon ground cumin
¾ teaspoon ground turmeric
½ teaspoon cayenne pepper
½ teaspoon sweet ground paprika
2 tomatoes, peeled and diced
2 tablespoons chopped fresh coriander (substitute mint if preferred)
1 tablespoon grated fresh ginger
1 teaspoon salt
1 large cauliflower, washed and broken into florets

Melt the butter in a large frying pan. Add the potatoes and fry until they are tender and lightly browned. Transfer the potatoes to a plate. Wipe out the pan and add the vegetable oil. When hot, but before it starts smoking, add the mustard seeds. Cover with a lid and shake the pan constantly until they pop.

Slip in the onion and brown it lightly. Reduce the heat and add the lemon juice, ground coriander, cumin, turmeric, cayenne pepper and paprika. Blend well, then add the tomatoes, fresh coriander, ginger and salt; if the mixture seems a little dry, add a tablespoon or so of water.

Add the cauliflower and potatoes and turn to coat them in the spicy mixture. Reduce the heat and cover tightly. Cook for 15 minutes or until the cauliflower is well impregnated with the spice mixture and cooked to your liking; stir occasionally. Transfer to a serving dish and serve hot or warmish.

Spices and chilli *have an important role in the Indian diet. Some spice combinations are known to warm the body and are popular in the north of India where the winters can be bitterly cold. A commonly used warming spice mixture is garam masala, which can contain black pepper, black cardamom, cinnamon and cloves. In hotter climes, cooling spices such as cumin, green cardamom and black mustard seed are used for the opposite effect.*

Many spices help digestion and it is common to find ginger and garlic used together, ginger because of its good digestive properties, and garlic because there is some evidence to suggest it helps lower the blood pressure which ginger raises as it warms the body.

Mustard seeds are useful as a preservative and turmeric is important as a blood purifier and for its antiseptic properties.

dark mystery Stirfry Spinach and Eggplant

SERVES 6

2 tablespoons vegetable oil
1 tablespoon each cumin, brown mustard and fenugreek seeds
1 large onion, finely chopped
4 cloves garlic, roughly chopped
½ teaspoon chilli powder (optional)
1 small eggplant (aubergine), cut into small cubes
1 medium tomato, skinned and chopped
½ teaspoon salt
250–300g spinach, trimmed, washed and chopped

Heat the oil in a pan over a medium heat and fry the seeds. Once the mustard seeds stop popping, add the onion and cook until it has softened, then add the garlic and chilli powder, if using. Cook for a few minutes then add the eggplant, chopped tomato and salt. Cook gently, stirring often, until the eggplant has softened. Add the spinach, lower the heat and cook for a few minutes more, stirring, until the spinach has wilted. Serve hot.

Stirfry Spinach and Eggplant

spice Indian Peas, Spuds and Mushrooms

SERVES 4–6

500g button mushrooms, trimmed
2 cups shelled fresh peas or frozen peas
2 tablespoons ghee or oil
1 medium onion, finely chopped
2 cloves garlic, crushed
1 tablespoon coarsely grated fresh ginger
3 tablespoons chopped fresh coriander
½ teaspoon chilli powder
1 teaspoon turmeric
1½ teaspoons salt
500g small waxy potatoes, scrubbed

Wipe the mushrooms clean or, if they are very gritty, wash them under running water and leave them to dry in a sieve.

If using frozen peas, tip them into a sieve and pour 2 cups of hot water over them. Leave to drain.

Heat the ghee or oil in a large frying pan over a low heat. Add the onion and garlic and cook for about 10 minutes or until lightly golden, stirring occasionally.

Squeeze the juice from the ginger over the onion and add the coriander. Cook for a minute, stirring, then add the chilli powder, turmeric and salt. Add the mushrooms, potatoes and fresh peas, if you are using them. Stir well, then pour ½ a cup of water in.

Cover with a tight-fitting lid, then simmer gently for 15 minutes. If using frozen peas, add them now. Cover again and cook for 15 minutes more or until the potatoes are tender. If there is too much liquid left, cook for a further 5–10 minutes, uncovered and stirring often, or, if the liquid dries up, add a little more. Serve hottish.

This is an intriguing earthy-toned dish full of flavour and texture. Serve it as part of an Indian all-vegetable meal, with a yoghurt-based dish. And remember, the important thing when using spices is that they must be fresh!

smoky Bharat's Dhal

SERVES 6–8

2 cups yellow split pea dhal
1½ teaspoons salt
1 teaspoon ground turmeric
3 fresh green chillies, halved and deseeded
10 curry leaves
1 teaspoon chilli powder, or to taste
1 tablespoon oil
3 small pieces dried red chilli or 3 tiny dried 'bird's eye' chillies
pinch of asafoetida powder (see page 80)
1 teaspoon black mustard seeds
1 teaspoon cumin seeds
3 cloves garlic, roughly chopped
½ onion, sliced
1 tablespoon fresh coriander leaves

Put the prepared dhal (see below) in a medium saucepan and pour in enough water to cover it by two-thirds. Bring to the boil and remove any scum. Add the salt and turmeric and cook gently, stirring often, for about 45 minutes, until the dhal is nearly tender. If the dhal is too thick at this stage, add more water. Add the fresh chillies, curry leaves and chilli powder and continue cooking until the dhal is mushy. Don't let it get too thick; add water if necessary.

In a small frying pan, heat the oil and add the dried chillies. When smoky, add the asafoetida, and mustard and cumin seeds. A few seconds after the popping ceases, add the garlic and onion. Brown the onion. A precaution – this is quite a volatile mixture. Add it to the dhal and immediately cover with a lid. Leave for 5 minutes then stir the coriander through.

This is a thickish soupy dhal which is good served with rice, tomato chutney and a meat or vegetable curry.

Curry leaves, which are easily grown, are said to be a tonic. Coriander leaves are said to have a cooling effect on the body. Both are popular garnishes and flavourings in Indo-Fijian cuisine.

It is wise to pick over dhals before cooking them, looking for tiny stones, and to rinse them well under running water to remove dust. Lentils are usually free of stones but they always need a good rinse to remove dust.

head-lifting Gujarati Eggplant and Potato Curry

SERVES 6

2 tablespoons oil
3 tiny dried 'bird's eye' chillies
$\frac{1}{8}$ teaspoon asafoetida powder
1 teaspoon black mustard seeds
1 tablespoon grated ginger
4–8 cloves garlic, crushed
5 fresh mild green chillies, deseeded and finely
   sliced
1 heaped teaspoon ground turmeric
1 teaspoon coarsely ground cumin
2 teaspoons coarsely ground coriander seeds
1 teaspoon chilli powder (optional – only if you
   want a head-lifter)
2 medium tomatoes, skinned and diced
$\frac{1}{4}$ onion, finely chopped
500g (3 large) waxy potatoes, peeled and cubed
500g (1 large or 2 medium) eggplants
   (aubergines), cubed
$1\frac{1}{2}$ teaspoons salt
1 tablespoon chopped fresh coriander leaves

Heat the oil in a medium-large saucepan and add the dried chillies. When smoky, add the asafoetida powder and mustard seeds. When the mustard seeds stop popping, add the ginger, garlic, green chillies, turmeric, cumin, coriander seeds and chilli powder, if using. Stirfry for a few minutes, then add the tomatoes, onion, potatoes, eggplants and salt. Stir well then cook gently for 10 minutes, covered with a lid; stir often to prevent sticking.

If the mixture is very dry (it probably will be) add $\frac{1}{2}$ cup of water.

Lower the heat, partially cover with a lid and cook gently until the vegetables are tender, approximately 40 minutes. Add the coriander leaves and let the curry rest for at least 10 minutes before serving.

This is a great *everyday vegetable curry typical of Indo-Fijian curries, given to me by colleague Bharat Jamnadas. The thinnish liquid shows its Gujarati heritage.*

Asafoetida *is a stinky little resin (aza = resin, foetidus = stinking) which is used in small quantities to help in the digestion of protein-rich foods, such as dhals and curds, and to help lessen flatulence. Keep it stored airtight – a packet of it will probably last longer than you!*

pumping Spicy Pumpkin

SERVES 4

2 tablespoons vegetable oil
1 teaspoon ground cumin
$\frac{1}{2}$ teaspoon chilli powder (optional)
1 teaspoon turmeric
3 cloves garlic, crushed
$\frac{1}{2}$ a large pumpkin, peeled, deseeded and cubed
$\frac{1}{2}$ cup water
$\frac{1}{2}$ teaspoon salt
freshly ground black pepper to taste
$\frac{1}{2}$ cup plain yoghurt
1 tablespoon finely chopped mint

Heat the oil in a frying pan and add spices and garlic. Cook gently for about 5 minutes, stirring, then add the pumpkin. Stir to coat the pumpkin in the spices, pour the water in and add the salt and black pepper.

Cover with a lid and cook gently until tender; approximately 15 minutes.

Transfer to a serving dish and spoon over the previously mixed yoghurt and mint.

Serve hottish or at room temperature (also good served cold the next day).

Gujarati Eggplant and Potato Curry

relieve

ease

cool

soothe

subdue

quell

calm

chill out *frosty*

icy

Spiced Watermelon

Eggplant with Yoghurt and Coriander

Coconut Yoghurt

Pumpkin Salad with Lime and Coriander

Cucumber and Peanut Salad

Watermelon and Ginger Sambal

tranquil

serenity

incandescent Spiced Watermelon

SERVES 6

1.5kg watermelon ($\frac{1}{2}$ a small oval watermelon)
2 cloves garlic, crushed
$\frac{1}{2}$ teaspoon salt
1 tablespoon oil
$1\frac{1}{2}$ teaspoons chilli powder
pinch of turmeric
$\frac{1}{2}$ teaspoon ground coriander seeds
$\frac{1}{4}$ teaspoon cumin seeds
$\frac{1}{4}$ teaspoon sugar to taste
1 tablespoon lime juice

Cut the watermelon into pieces, flick out all the seeds and cut off the rind, then cut the watermelon into large cubes. Purée 1 cup of cubes in a liquidiser or food processor with the garlic and salt.

Heat the oil in a large frying pan and add the chilli powder, turmeric, coriander and cumin seeds. Stirfry for 30 seconds, then add the watermelon purée. Cook gently for 5 minutes, then add the sugar and lime juice. Cook for 1 minute, then add the watermelon cubes, and cook gently for a few minutes more until warmed through. Turn into a bowl and serve warm, or, alternatively, serve chilled.

Steeping watermelon in a spicy bath of chilli and spice seeds turns it into an incandescent marvel. I like it served chilled as a curry cooler, but it's also good as a juicy, hot and sour side salad with cold duck.

Spiced Watermelon

pockets Eggplant with Yoghurt and Coriander

SERVES 8

2 medium eggplants (aubergines)
$\frac{3}{4}$ teaspoon salt
$\frac{1}{4}$ teaspoon chilli powder
1 clove garlic, crushed
2 tablespoons chopped coriander
200ml plain yoghurt

Pierce the eggplants in several places with a skewer, then put them on an oven rack in an oven preheated to 200°C. Bake for about 40 minutes or until very tender. Transfer them to a plate and leave to cool. (The eggplants can be cooked a day before required; keep refrigerated.)

Cut the eggplants in half lengthways and scoop out the flesh with a teaspoon. Discard the skins. Drain the flesh in a sieve for 30 minutes, then transfer it to a bowl and mash with a fork. Mix in the salt, chilli powder, garlic, coriander and yoghurt. Chill before serving.

Cooking eggplants *over hot coals gives them an amazing rich, smoky flavour – but it is more convenient for most people to cook them in the oven. Serve this dish with Indian foods, as a yoghurty-dip sort of dish, scooping it up with warm, soft roti. Alternatively, serve it with flash-fried or barbecued chunks of lamb or chicken, stuffed into warm puffy pita breads, with salady bits on the side.*

chill Coconut Yoghurt

SERVES 6-8

4 tablespoons freshly grated coconut
2 cloves garlic, chopped
1 tablespoon chopped onion
1 green chilli, deseeded and roughly chopped
few pinches salt
$\frac{1}{4}$ teaspoon sugar
2 cups plain yoghurt

Put the coconut, garlic, onion, chilli, salt and sugar with $\frac{1}{2}$ cup of the yoghurt in a food processor and process until finely blended. Add the rest of the yoghurt and process. If it is too thick, thin with a little milk. Chill.

Chilli can burn *the mouth, but it has a cooling effect on the body. Initially, a burst of hot chilli makes you feel like a dragon belching fire, and your body breaks out in a sweat. As the sweat dries on the skin, it gives a cooling sensation, then it leaves you in a tranquil state. That's why people in hot countries eat such hot curries – it keeps them cool!*

It is advisable to wear disposable plastic gloves when preparing chillies because the capsaicin around the seeds can irritate your skin.

The chilli can be omitted from this dish or any other recipes in this book if you want a sweeter taste.

Eggplant with Yoghurt and Coriander

sublime Pumpkin Salad with Lime and Coriander

SERVES 6–8

$\frac{1}{2}$ **a large firm-fleshed pumpkin**
salt
$1\frac{1}{4}$ cups plain yoghurt
1 tablespoon sweet mango chutney (use the liquid part only)
1 teaspoon fresh lime juice
1 fresh hot red chilli, halved, deseeded and very finely chopped
2 tablespoons coarsely chopped coriander leaves (or use mint for a change)

GARNISH
1 fresh hot red chilli
a few sprigs of fresh coriander
twirl of lime rind

Cut the pumpkin into large chunks, chop out the seeds then peel it. Either steam or gently boil the pumpkin in salted water until it is nearly tender. Cool, then cut the pumpkin into large cubes. Pile it up in a dish.

In a bowl mix together the yoghurt, chutney, lime juice, chilli, coriander and $\frac{1}{4}$ teaspoon of salt. Just prior to serving, pour the dressing over the pumpkin. Garnish with the chilli, chopped coriander and lime zest.

The sweet, delicate nutty flavour of good firm-fleshed pumpkin lends itself to sweet and sour treatments (Italian style, with red wine vinegar, mint and garlic, is a knock-out) and to tangy spicy dishes like this one. But the result is quite different when it is steamed, mashed, roasted, sautéed, stuffed, used as a stuffing for pasta or made into soup, and that's its real asset – versatility. It can also be stored for a long time. Steaming the pumpkin, rather than boiling it, will produce a better result, keeping the texture firmer and the flesh drier. Take care not to overcook it in this recipe, otherwise you'll have mash on your hands. Try this as a sambal with Indian foods.

Pumpkin Salad with Lime and Coriander

sweet Cucumber and Peanut Salad

SERVES 6

½ **cup raw peanuts**
1 **long telegraph cucumber**
1 **teaspoon white sugar**
4 **tablespoons white vinegar**
2 **fresh hot red chillies, deseeded and very finely chopped**
2 **shallots (eschallots), finely sliced**
2 **tablespoons chopped mint**
fish sauce (optional)

Put the peanuts in a shallow ovenproof dish. Roast them for about 12 minutes or until browned, in an oven preheated to 200°C. When cool, crush with a rolling pin or in a mortar with a pestle, until coarsely chopped.

Trim and peel the cucumber, slice in half lengthways and scoop out the seeds with a teaspoon. Slice cucumber thinly and put in a bowl. Dissolve the sugar in the vinegar, pour over the cucumber and toss well.

Scatter the chopped chillies, shallots and mint over the cucumber and toss well. Scatter the peanuts over, then sprinkle with a few drops of fish sauce, if using. Serve immediately.

If you want to make this ahead, get everything ready, but don't mix it until the last minute. Serve with Thai dishes or with simple grilled, baked or barbecued fish.

shiver Watermelon and Ginger Sambal

SERVES 6

2kg watermelon (approximately ½ a large watermelon)
1 **tablespoon grated ginger**
1 **tablespoon vegetable oil**
a few pinches of salt
1 **tablespoon finely chopped mint**

Cut the watermelon in two, flick out as many seeds as possible then roll it into balls with a melon-baller, flicking out seeds as you go. Alternatively, cut the watermelon into small cubes. Put the watermelon balls or cubes, and any juice, into a bowl. Squeeze the juice from the ginger into the bowl with the other ingredients. Toss, cover and chill for at least 2 hours before serving.

Watermelon is one of the most refreshing fruits there is. It is particularly good chilled on a hot day, eaten as a fruit or turned into a slushy ice, which is a great reviver. It also makes interesting salads and sambals. Although this fruit is about 90% water, it also contains some Vitamin A and C and calcium, plus significant amounts of phosphorus.

essential

verve

nouri

satisfy

thrive

punchy

crucial

powerhouse

vital *vigour*

carbo-load

s h

Puy Lentils with Lemon Oil

Flageolet Bean Salad

White Bean, Fennel and Mint Salad

Pumpkin, Red Onion and Tomato Gratin

Gingered Cabbage and Zucchini

Roasted Mediterranean Medley

Gujarati Cabbage and Peanut Salad

White Beans with Peppers and Parmesan

Crisp Vegetables with Mustard Seeds

alive

flourish

infuse

Puy Lentils with Lemon Oil

SERVES 6

1 fresh bay leaf
parsley stalks
1 sage leaf
strip of orange peel
2 tablespoons extra virgin olive oil
1 large shallot (eschallot), chopped (about 3
   tablespoons chopped shallot)
1 small clove garlic, crushed
250g puy lentils, picked over and washed
1½ cups water
½ teaspoon salt
freshly ground black pepper to taste
3 tablespoons lemon-infused extra virgin olive oil
strips of lemon peel and fresh bay leaves to
   garnish

Tie the bay leaf, parsley stalks, sage leaf and strip of orange peel together with string.

Put the extra virgin olive oil in a saucepan with the shallot and garlic. Cover with a lid and cook gently for 5 minutes or until soft. Stir in the lentils and add the tied bundle of flavourings. Pour in the water.

Slowly bring to the boil, turn the heat to low and cook gently for 25–40 minutes or until tender, adding a little more water if necessary. (The liquid should have evaporated by the end of cooking; remove the lid and reduce if too moist.)

Discard the flavourings, mix in the salt and black pepper and tip the lentils into a bowl. Drizzle the lemon-infused olive oil over, garnish with a few strips of lemon peel and a fresh bay leaf or two. Leave for 10 minutes before serving.

Pulses are the edible seeds of leguminous plants, which include peas, beans and lentils. Lentils are round and flattish in shape and vary in size and colour and they can be sold whole or skinned and split. Many lentils go by their Indian names as various dhals (alternative spellings: dahl, dal). They have been cultivated since prehistoric times. They're a valuable and inexpensive source of protein and contain good amounts of iron, calcium, potassium and the B vitamins thiamine and nicotinic acid. They are low in fat, high in dietary fibre and carbohydrates and are easily digested. Vitamin C is produced if the lentils are sprouted. (Sprout them only until the growth is the same length as the seed.)

Lentils and beans are an excellent source of protein, but the protein is incomplete (unlike meat which has complete protein). However, around 30% more of the protein is made available to the body if the lentils are eaten with cereal. Some of the oldest dishes in the world are based on this knowledge (for example Indian dhals with rice or with Indian breads, Middle Eastern dishes of chick peas and grains, even baked beans on toast).

They are particularly important in the vegetarian diet. Lentils eaten at the same meal with rice and bread and a dairy product, such as yoghurt or cheese, will yield as much protein as red meat.

French lentilles vertes du puy are small, dark greeny brown lentils. They are protected by an 'appellation d'origine', in the same way fine wines are. They are highly sought after because they retain their shape after cooking and have a chewy texture and a nutty, earthy taste. They are great with turkey, poussins, quail, pigeon, pheasant, guinea fowl, or, if you're a vegetarian, with other vegetable dishes.

pulse  Flageolet Bean Salad

SERVES 6

200g dried flageolet beans
1 fresh bay leaf
1 large sprig thyme
2 tablespoons extra virgin olive oil
1 teaspoon salt
freshly ground black pepper to taste
2 tablespoons coarsely chopped parsley
1 small clove garlic, crushed
1 small shallot (eschallot), very finely chopped
2 large tomatoes, halved, deseeded, diced and drained

Put the beans in a bowl and cover with plenty of boiling water. Leave to soak for several hours. Drain, rinse and put them in a saucepan. Cover generously with boiling water and bring to the boil. Remove any scum from the surface of the water, then add the bay leaf and thyme. Lower the heat, cover with a lid and cook at a gentle boil for 1–2 hours or until tender (test regularly after the first hour of cooking). Alternatively, cook in a pressure cooker.

Drain the beans when tender and drape a piece of absorbent kitchen paper over the top of them to prevent the surface from drying out while they cool.

Mix the oil, salt, black pepper, parsley, garlic, shallot and tomatoes together in a bowl, then pour the mixture over the flageolet beans. Toss well and leave at room temperature for an hour before serving.

Generally the only pulses which don't require soaking before cooking are lentils and split peas. Most other beans and peas are best soaked before cooking to allow them to fully rehydrate, to shorten the cooking time and to make them more digestible. If you live in an area with hard water on tap, it is best to soak the pulses in boiled water. (Boiling the water drives off the calcium carbonate in the steam. Pulses that absorb calcium carbonate take longer to cook.) Using bicarbonate to soften the water is outmoded because it destroys Vitamin B1.

Beans are a nutritious food, rich in calcium, phosphorus, iron and vitamins from the B group, but like lentils, their protein is incomplete (see Pulses, page 94).

Flageolet beans are slim, elongated beans, pale green or cream in colour (there are always some of both colour in a bag of beans). They are good in a salad because they hold their shape well, but they are also fantastic served hot with a roasted leg of lamb imbued with the fragrance of rosemary. In the mouth they are smooth and slippery until you bite them and the fluffy, nutty-tasting interior of the beans bursts out.

It is hard to estimate how long it will take to cook the beans, but in this dish they can be cooked several hours before serving.

gutsy White Bean, Fennel and Mint Salad

SERVES 8–10

400g dried white beans, soaked for several hours in plenty of cold water
1 large stalk celery, halved
1 large leek, trimmed and cut into thirds
1 large carrot, quartered
a few parsley stalks
1 fresh bay leaf
2 cloves garlic, crushed
1 tablespoon Dijon mustard
$\frac{3}{4}$ teaspoon salt
3 tablespoons white wine vinegar
125ml extra virgin olive oil
2 tablespoons chopped mint
2 tablespoons chopped parsley
2 small bulbs fennel
juice of 1 lemon, strained

Put the drained beans in a saucepan. Add the celery, leek, carrot, parsley stalks and bay leaf. Cover generously with cold water, bring to the boil, then cook gently, partially covered, until just tender. Drain. Remove the vegetables and herbs (see below).

In a food processor put the garlic, mustard, salt, vinegar and 2 tablespoons of the beans. Process, then blend in the oil.

Turn the beans into a bowl and pour the dressing over. Toss gently. When cool, add the mint and parsley. Cover and refrigerate until required (overnight is fine).

Just before serving, trim the fennel and slice it thinly. Put it in a bowl with the lemon juice. Toss well. Gently toss the beans, transfer them to a serving bowl and top with the fennel.

If you have *a baby, mash the discarded vegetables with a little of the cooking liquor – baby will love it. If you have a toddler, add a few mashed beans as well. And if you happen to have an Italian in the family, of course they'll scoff up the vegetables and a spoonful of beans anointed with a few drops of the finest extra virgin olive oil, salt and black pepper, as a little snackette.*

This is a wonderful dish to serve with roast pork or a whole baked fish.

baked Pumpkin, Red Onion and Tomato Gratin

SERVES 8

$\frac{1}{2}$ a large firm-fleshed pumpkin
500g (about 8) plum tomatoes, sliced (these tomatoes hold their shape better)
300g (3) red onions, sliced
1$\frac{1}{2}$ teaspoons finely chopped rosemary
3 large cloves garlic, chopped
salt
freshly ground black pepper to taste
extra virgin olive oil

Cut the pumpkin into large chunks and chop out the seeds. Peel the pumpkin then slice it thinly. Put it in a large gratin dish or smallish roasting dish, then put the tomatoes and onions on top (don't arrange them). Scatter the rosemary and garlic over, sprinkle with salt and grind on some black pepper.

Drizzle generously with oil, then bake the gratin for about 45 minutes in an oven preheated to 200°C, or until the pumpkin is just tender and the top is browned. Serve hottish or at room temperature.

This goes well *with roasted chicken and a crispy green salad with a good vinaigrette. Alternatively, serve it as a main course vegetable dish, with a spinach salad and large baked or barbecued mushrooms flavoured with a few sprigs of thyme and a drizzle of extra virgin olive oil.*

addictive Gingered Cabbage and Zucchini

SERVES 4–6

1 tablespoon peanut oil
1 teaspoon sesame oil
2 cloves garlic, crushed
1 tablespoon coarsely grated ginger
½ a small white or Savoy cabbage, core cut out, rinsed and thinly sliced
2 yellow or green zucchini (courgettes), thinly sliced
2 tablespoons chopped coriander
½ cup dry-roasted peanuts
1 tablespoon sesame seeds, toasted in a dry pan
¼ teaspoon salt
grated rind and juice of 1 lemon

Put the peanut and sesame oils in a hot wok set over a high heat. When the oils are hot, add the garlic and ginger and stirfry for a few seconds until fragrant. Quickly add the cabbage and zucchini and stirfry until the cabbage is just starting to wilt.

Quickly mix the coriander, peanuts, sesame seeds, salt and lemon rind and juice through the cabbage. Tip into a serving bowl and serve immediately.

fast-cook Roasted Mediterranean Medley

SERVES 4–6

2 leeks
2 yellow zucchini (courgettes) or scallopini
2 green zucchini (courgettes) or scallopini
6 baby eggplants (aubergines) or 6 long Japanese (ladyfinger) eggplants
1 tablespoon pesto
2 tablespoons extra virgin olive oil
½ teaspoon salt
freshly ground black pepper to taste
small piece of Italian parmesan cheese, cut into curls with a vegetable peeler

Trim the leeks and wash well, then cut into chunks 2–3cm wide. Cut the zucchini into chunks. If using scallopini, cut in half horizontally, or leave baby ones whole. Trim and cut the eggplants in half lengthways.

Mix the pesto in a large bowl with the oil, salt and some black pepper. Put all the vegetables in the bowl and toss them well to coat in the dressing. Leave to marinate for 30 minutes.

Spread the vegetables in a large shallow baking dish (preferably non-stick) or a baking tray lined with baking paper.

Cook for 15 minutes in an oven preheated to 220°C. Remove the tray from the oven and turn the vegetables over with tongs. Return to the oven and bake the vegetables for about 15 minutes more or until tender and well browned. Transfer to a platter, garnish with the parmesan curls and serve hottish.

A tray of fast-cooked vegetables makes the ideal central dish for an all-vegetable meal. I like the idea too, because it's simple to prepare (use any combination of vegetables you have) and easy to cook. Try this combination with a tomato and black olive salad, crusty bread and a tumble of hot cooked sweet corn sliced off the cobs.

Roasted Mediterranean Medley

green leaves Gujarati Cabbage

and Peanut Salad

SERVES 6

2 tablespoons peanut oil

2 teaspoons mustard seeds

2 fresh hot green chillies, halved, deseeded and
very finely chopped

small piece of ginger, peeled and grated

15 fresh curry leaves

2 carrots peeled then cut into very thin strips
with a vegetable peeler

$\frac{1}{2}$ a small white or Savoy cabbage, core cut out,
rinsed and thinly sliced

salt

freshly ground black pepper to taste

grated zest and juice of 1 lime

1 teaspoon sugar

2 tablespoons chopped coriander

$\frac{1}{2}$ cup peanuts, roasted

Heat the oil in a wok set over a high heat. Put in the mustard seeds and as soon as they finish popping, add the chillies, ginger, curry leaves and carrots. Stirfry for 2 minutes, then add the cabbage. Stirfry for a few minutes more, until the cabbage just starts to wilt. Quickly season with salt and black pepper, stir the lime zest, lime juice, sugar and coriander through the cabbage. Turn into a serving bowl and scatter the peanuts over the top. Serve immediately.

In our society, cabbage is a much underrated vegetable, but in several cultures it's an integral part of a sustaining diet (German sauerkraut and Korean kimchi, for example). I love finding new ways of adding it to the menu because it's such a health-giving vegetable, containing phytochemicals, which help fight cancers.

Cabbage is delicious raw in salads, possessing an addictive peppery taste and pleasant crunch. Lightly steamed, stirfried or sautéed with herbs and spices, it's a tasty, nutritious, quickly cooked vegetable. That terrible smell we all hate comes from overcooking it. Cooking it until it has just wilted, or quickly cooking it in hot oil, is the way to treat it. Remember the green leaves contain the most nutrients. Cabbage also provides useful amounts of calcium and potassium.

Gujarati Cabbage and Peanut Salad

caper White Beans with Peppers and Parmesan

SERVES 6

1 cup dried white beans (or use chick peas)
1.5 litres water
1 teaspoon white wine vinegar
3 large cloves garlic, crushed
1 tablespoon capers, drained
75ml extra virgin olive oil
$\frac{1}{2}$ cup freshly grated Italian parmesan cheese
2 tablespoons olive oil
1 large onion, sliced
1 large red pepper (capsicum), halved, cored, deseeded and chopped
$\frac{1}{2}$ cup black olives, halved and stoned
12 basil leaves
1 teaspoon tomato paste
$\frac{1}{4}$ teaspoon salt
freshly ground black pepper to taste

Soak the beans for several hours in cold water to cover. Drain and tip into a saucepan. Pour in the measured water and bring to the boil. Lower the heat, remove any scum from the surface, then partially cover with a lid. Cook at a gentle boil for about 40 minutes or until just tender; be careful not to overcook them.

Put the vinegar, 1 clove of garlic and the capers in a bowl. Whisk in the extra virgin olive oil and parmesan. When the beans are ready, drain them and tip into a serving bowl. Pour on the dressing and toss well.

Put the olive oil in a frying pan, add the onion, remaining garlic and red pepper. Cook over a medium-low heat for 10 minutes or until the onion is soft, stirring often. Add the olives, basil leaves, tomato paste, salt and black pepper. Cook for 5 minutes more, then spoon over the dressed beans. Mix very gently together (just two or three stirs), then leave at room temperature until cool. Either serve cool, or cover and refrigerate until required.

This makes an *excellent main course vegetarian dish. I'd team it up with a crusty loaf of ciabatta bread (Italian sour dough loaf shaped like a flattish slipper) and a rocket salad.*

For information on capers, see page 15.

chillied Crisp Vegetables with Mustard Seeds

SERVES 6

3 tablespoons peanut oil
$\frac{1}{2}$ teaspoon fenugreek seeds
$\frac{3}{4}$ teaspoon black mustard seeds
1 tablespoon grated ginger
1 large clove garlic, crushed
$\frac{1}{4}$ teaspoon chilli powder
1 teaspoon turmeric
250g slim green beans, topped and tailed (if long, cut beans into short lengths; if very thick, slit lengthways first)
$\frac{1}{2}$ a small cauliflower, cut into small florets
3 good-sized carrots, peeled and cut into thinnish sticks
$\frac{1}{4}$ cup water
$\frac{1}{2}$ teaspoon salt

Heat a large wok over a medium-high heat for a few minutes, then pour in the oil. When it is hot, put in the fenugreek and mustard seeds. Cook briefly until the mustard seeds pop, then add the ginger, garlic, chilli powder and turmeric. Stirfry for 1–2 minutes, then add the vegetables.

Lower the heat to medium, stirfry for 5 minutes, then add the water and the salt. Cover with a lid and cook for approximately 5 minutes more, stirring often, or until crisp-tender (add more water if it evaporates before the vegetables are done to your liking). Turn into a heated dish and serve immediately.

Like broccoli, *cauliflower contains folate, potassium, calcium, Vitamins C and K, and B group vitamins, and it is also believed to play a role in fighting cancers. More of the nutrients are stored in the stem than in the florets, so try to use the stems too.*

Always buy fresh snow-white cauliflowers with compact heads. Limp, browning cauliflowers not only smell but will also have lost much of their nutritional goodness. Raw crisp cauliflower makes an excellent salad, either doused in a garlicky, mustardy vinaigrette sharpened with vinegar, or in a caper mayonnaise.

Crisp Vegetables with Mustard Seeds

contentment

bliss

comf

hearten

cozy

cheer

warming

ample

ease

satisfaction

ort

Baby Beetroot with Cream and Chives

Witloof, Watercress and Orange Salad

Garlicky Beans with Cashew Nuts

Radicchio Salad

Parsnip Crisps

Sautéed Brussels Sprout Leaves

Braised Red Cabbage and Apples

Roasted Roots

Gratin of Potatoes and Celeriac

Sweet Potatoes with Pine Nuts, Currants and Mint

Endive Salad with Walnuts

Hot Buttered Cucumber

Gratin of Winter Vegetables

Porcini Mushroom Risotto

Garbure Basque

Leek, Bacon and Potato Soup

Potato Cake

snug

familiar

beet Baby Beetroot with Cream and Chives

SERVES 6

700g baby beetroot or 6 medium ones
$\frac{1}{2}$ cup cream
2 tablespoons snipped chives
salt
freshly ground black pepper to taste
lemon wedges (optional)

Wash the beetroot without tearing the skin. Trim the leaves and the tapering root if they are very long, but don't cut the beetroot flesh or the beetroot will bleed during cooking. Put the beetroot in a saucepan and cover generously with cold water. Bring to the boil, then lower the heat, partially cover with a lid and cook gently until tender (the skin will slip off easily when they are tender); allow 20–30 minutes for baby beetroot and about 45 minutes for large ones.

Drain, then remove the stalks, tapering roots and skin. Leave whole or cut into quarters or slices. The beetroot can be prepared ahead to this point and either reheated briefly in the microwave, or in the oven covered with a lid, for about 15 minutes.

About 5 minutes before serving, put the cream in a saucepan and bring to the boil. Reduce by half, then sprinkle the chives over, add a few pinches of salt and grind on some black pepper. Arrange the hot beetroot in a heated serving dish and spoon the creamy chive dressing over. Serve immediately, with lemon wedges if using.

It's worth growing *a patch of baby beetroot, even if you don't harvest the beets, because the leaves are very nutritious and, when young and sweet, they are very tender. Use the leaves raw in salads (try a mix of baby beetroot leaves, cos lettuce, orange segments and toasted, salted almonds with a lemon vinaigrette), or they can be quickly stirfried or chopped and used in stuffings.*

peppy Witloof, Watercress and Orange Salad

SERVES 8

2 large juicy oranges
2 bunches watercress
6 witloof (Belgian endive) or 1 large curly endive, washed, dried and torn into bite-sized pieces
3 tablespoons extra virgin olive oil
1 tablespoon tarragon vinegar
$\frac{1}{4}$ teaspoon salt
freshly ground black pepper to taste

Prepare the oranges as on page 54. Don't waste the juice in the membrane; squeeze it and drink it!

Wash and pick over the watercress, discarding thick stalks, then spin it dry in a salad spinner.

The salad can be prepared ahead to this point; put the greens in a plastic bag and refrigerate until required.

Trim the ends of the witloof and remove any damaged leaves. Slice into chunks, separating the leaves. Place in a bowl with the oranges and watercress.

In a bowl mix the oil, vinegar, salt and black pepper, then pour it over the salad. Toss well and serve.

Watercress is excellent *in salads, providing a peppery bite. It's extremely good for you and there are plenty of other ways of including it in the diet. It makes an interesting filling for sandwiches, panini and pita pockets, is good in egg dishes, particularly omelettes, and adds taste to tarts and quiches. Buy only bright green sprightly watercress and use it the day you buy it.*

thyme Garlicky Beans with Cashew Nuts

SERVES 4

400g green beans, topped and tailed, or a mixture of green and butter beans
Maldon sea salt
2 tablespoons extra virgin olive oil
50g raw cashew nuts
1 large clove garlic, crushed
freshly ground black pepper to taste
1 teaspoon chopped thyme (or winter savory)

Plunge the beans into a saucepan of boiling salted water and cook, uncovered, for 3–5 minutes or until crisp-tender. Drain, then dry on absorbent kitchen paper. If using butter beans, cook them separately, for 2 minutes only.

Heat the oil in a large frying pan over a medium heat, then add the cashew nuts. Fry until the nuts turn a pale golden brown, stirring often with a slotted spoon. Transfer the cashew nuts to a side plate.

Tip the beans and garlic into the pan and cook for several minutes, stirring often, until the garlic is brown and nutty smelling.

Sprinkle with a little salt and grind on some black pepper. Toss once or twice more, mix in the cashews and thyme, and transfer to a heated serving bowl. Serve immediately.

craving Radicchio Salad

SERVES 4–6

1 teaspoon white wine vinegar
1 tablespoon capers, drained
1 clove garlic, crushed
1 tablespoon coarsely chopped parsley
$\frac{1}{2}$ cup extra virgin olive oil
$\frac{1}{2}$ cup (50g) freshly grated Italian parmesan cheese
3–6 radicchio lettuces (use 3 large or 6 small ones)

Blend the vinegar, capers, garlic and parsley together in a food processor fitted with the chopping blade. While the machine is running, dribble in the oil, then stop the machine, scatter the parmesan over and process briefly until blended. The dressing can be prepared several hours ahead to this point; store it covered at room temperature. Alternatively, make it by hand – blend all the ingredients, except the oil, in a bowl with a fork, then slowly mix in the oil.

Wash and dry the radicchio, then tear into bite-sized pieces and put in a salad bowl. Pour the dressing over, toss very well then serve. Although the salad is at its best when first dressed, leftovers are delicious too.

I'm addicted to this salad. I adore radicchio anyway, and crave its bitter edge with certain dishes. The chemistry of these ingredients, though, changes things dramatically. It's sharpened with vinegar and capers, seasoned with piquant parmesan, smoothed and soothed with extra virgin olive oil and given a kick-along with garlic and grassy tasting parsley.

Garlicky Beans with Cashew Nuts

crunchy Parsnip Crisps

SERVES 4

4 large parsnips
oil for frying
Maldon sea salt

Peel the parsnips, trim, then shave into long, thin strips with a potato peeler. Fry in batches in hot oil in a deep-fryer until lightly golden. Remove from the oil with tongs, drain briefly on absorbent kitchen paper and sprinkle with salt. Cool, then store airtight. The crisps can be made several hours in advance.

Like turnips, parsnips have been grown since Roman times. The parsnip is a root vegetable, and along with carrot and parsley, it belongs to the Umbelliferae family. Not surprisingly, the three ingredients work well together. Choose medium-sized specimens, because large ones will have woody centres which need to be cut out. The best have had an early morning shiver or two in frosty fields, which sweetens them somewhat. The smell and taste can best be described as earthy and sweet, and slightly nutty. They roast well, and can be mashed, steamed, sautéed, made into crisps or chips, or turned into a soup or soufflé. One of the most remarkable soups using this vegetable is a simple blend of onions softened in butter seasoned with a generous spoonful of curry powder, plenty of parsnips and chicken stock, all cooked together until tender, then puréed and finished off with cream. Buy nice taut parsnips, not softened or wizened ones. Parsnips contain traces of some of the B vitamins, Vitamin C and potassium.

perky Sautéed Brussels Sprout Leaves

SERVES 6

Brussels sprouts (allow about 3 per person)
salt
butter
freshly ground black pepper to taste
a few gratings of fresh nutmeg

Trim the Brussels sprouts, then peel off the leaves, trimming more off the bottom when you can no longer peel away any more leaves; the very tiny ones in the centre of each sprout will be unusable.

When all the Brussels sprouts are prepared, rinse the leaves. Plunge them into a large saucepan of boiling salted water and cook, uncovered, for 3–4 minutes or until nearly tender. Drain and rinse well with cold water until the leaves feel cool (this helps to keep their green colour). Shake well and leave to drain.

The leaves can be prepared 1–2 hours ahead to this point; keep them at room temperature, uncovered.

Five minutes before serving, heat a large frying pan or wok with a large knob of butter over a low heat. Melt the butter, then drop in the leaves. Stirfry until very hot but still crisp-tender. If the leaves start to catch on the bottom of the pan, add a tablespoon of stock or water (they mustn't fry or they will lose colour).

Sprinkle with a little salt, grind on some black pepper and nutmeg and tip into a serving dish. Serve immediately (don't cover).

Look for green, compact Brussels sprouts – soft yellowish ones are not worth buying. Like broccoli, Brussels sprouts are packed with goodies – plenty of Vitamin C, some B vitamins and potassium, and, it's claimed, they help to prevent some cancers. Tight, perky little buds, especially if they've had a fright of frost, are crisp and tender enough to slice finely and use as a salad; mix with orange segments, mustard, salt, black pepper and extra virgin olive oil. Separating the leaves, as in this recipe, makes what is often a maligned vegetable, positively charming!

sharp tart Braised Red Cabbage and Apples

SERVES 6

1 large, firm red cabbage
large knob of butter
2 tart cooking apples
$\frac{1}{2}$ teaspoon salt
1 tablespoon castor sugar
1 tablespoon malt vinegar or white wine vinegar

Cut the cabbage in half with a sharp knife. Slice out the hard core, discard the outer leaves, then wash the cabbage under running water. Shake dry. Chop coarsely.

Rub the butter around the insides of a heavy-based casserole or saucepan and add half the cabbage. Peel and core the apples, slice them finely and arrange on top of the cabbage. Put in the rest of the cabbage, then sprinkle the salt, castor sugar and vinegar over. Cover with a tight-fitting lid and set on a medium heat.

When the cabbage is steaming and nearly boiling, turn the heat to low and cook very gently for 30 minutes. Quickly lift off the lid, letting clinging moisture drop onto the cabbage, turn the mixture with tongs and check the liquid level. If there is less than 2 tablespoons of liquid, add 1–2 tablespoons of water (don't be tempted to flood the cabbage; provide just enough liquid to prevent it catching on the bottom of the pan). Cook for 30 minutes more or until soft and very tender. Serve hot or at room temperature.

An alternative cooking method is to cook the cabbage in an oven preheated to 170°C for about an hour.

Red cabbage *can be tricky to cook well. If you cook it in 'hard' water (water with a high alkaline level) it will lose its red colour and turn an unattractive bluey-green. Adding acid (vinegar, lemon, tart fruits) corrects this and the cabbage remains a good red colour.*

rev-up Roasted Roots

SERVES 4–6

3 tablespoons olive oil
2 cloves garlic, chopped
1 teaspoon salt
freshly ground black pepper to taste
1 teaspoon chopped thyme
12 fresh sage leaves
6 fresh bay leaves
2 large baking potatoes (use old starchy potatoes, not freshly dug or 'new' potatoes), peeled and quartered
2 red onions, peeled and quartered
4 small carrots, trimmed (if the carrots are large, cut in half lengthways)
2 small turnips, peeled and quartered

Mix the oil, garlic, salt, black pepper and herbs in a large bowl. Add the vegetables and toss well to coat in the dressing. Leave to marinate for 30 minutes.

Arrange the vegetables in a large, shallow baking dish, positioning the onions and turnips in the centre of the dish and the potatoes and carrots around the edge.

Cook for 15 minutes in an oven preheated to 220°C. Remove the tray from the oven and turn the vegetables over with tongs. Return to the oven and bake the vegetables for about 15 minutes more or until tender and browned. Serve hottish.

Give classic roasted vegetables *a make-over. Rub them with olive oil, garlic, herbs and seasonings and roast on high until they surrender to the heat; crisp at the edges while keeping their moist or fluffy centres. If you've got a turnip phobia, exchange them for more carrots. Serve the roasted roots with vegetarian dishes or with a French-style casserole or sauté of chicken.*

Roasted Roots

saucy Gratin of Potatoes and Celeriac

SERVES 8

900g even-sized waxy potatoes, peeled
salt
1 celeriac root, approximately 400g
2 tablespoons lemon juice
500g (5–6 medium) plum tomatoes, peeled
2 tablespoons extra virgin olive oil
1 large clove garlic, crushed
$\frac{1}{2}$ cup cream
$\frac{1}{4}$ cup light stock
freshly ground black pepper to taste
butter for greasing the dish
150g gruyère cheese, grated

Put the potatoes in a large saucepan, cover with water, salt well and bring to the boil. Partially cover with a lid, then cook gently until just tender. Drain. When cool enough to handle, slice finely.

Peel the celeriac with a sharp knife, then slice thinly. Drop into a saucepan of boiling water, adding the lemon juice. Cook gently until nearly tender (about 12 minutes). Drain.

Cut the tomatoes in half, discard the cores and flick out the seeds. Chop finely. Put the oil in a large frying pan and set over a medium-high heat. When the oil is hot, quickly add the tomatoes and garlic.

Cook, stirring often, for 5 minutes, then pour in the cream and stock. Bubble up and cook for 2–3 minutes, then remove from the heat. Grind on plenty of black pepper.

Generously butter a large gratin dish (capacity approximately 1.5 litres). Arrange the potatoes in the dish, slightly overlapping. Sprinkle with half the cheese, then cover with a layer of celeriac.

The dish can be prepared several hours in advance to this point. Cover and refrigerate the gratin. Put the tomato sauce and cheese into containers, cover and refrigerate. Bring everything to room temperature before cooking the gratin.

Spoon the tomato sauce over the celeriac, then top with the rest of the cheese. Bake in an oven preheated to 200°C for about 45 minutes or until bubbling and golden brown on top. Serve hottish.

Celeriac is a swollen tuber, related to celery, but it's sweeter and milder to taste, with a hint of earthiness. It can be eaten raw, either grated or shredded finely, or cooked and made into a gratin, a mash or used in soups. Slice off all the thick skin with a sharp knife and either rub the cut celeriac with lemon juice, or blanch it in water to which has been added the juice of a lemon, to stop discolouration. Celeriac is available during cooler months and it can be stored for several weeks in the refrigerator.

Gratin of Potatoes and Celeriac

toasty Sweet Potatoes with Pine Nuts, Currants and Mint

SERVES 6

2 tablespoons currants
3 tablespoons red wine
800g sweet potatoes, peeled and cut into even-sized smallish cubes
salt
90ml water
2 tablespoons redcurrant jelly
generous 2 tablespoons chopped fresh mint (chop just before using)
knob of butter
freshly ground black pepper to taste
2 tablespoons pine nuts, lightly toasted in a dry frying pan

Put the currants in a small saucepan, pour the wine over and leave to soak for an hour or so.

Put the cubed sweet potatoes in a steaming basket or metal colander and set it over a saucepan of boiling water. Sprinkle with salt, cover with a lid or aluminium foil and steam over medium-high heat for 7–10 minutes or until just tender.

Add the water to the soaking currants and bring to the boil. Lower the heat and simmer very gently for 5 minutes. Add the redcurrant jelly, stir until dissolved then, lastly, add the mint.

Meanwhile, remove the steaming basket from the saucepan. Shake the sweet potatoes once or twice and turn them into a heated dish. Dot the butter over and grind on plenty of black pepper. Pour the redcurrant glaze over the sweet potatoes, scatter the pine nuts on top and serve immediately.

Sweet potatoes make a great mash, can be used successfully in soups, are terrific in salads (see Sweet Potato Salad, page 54), can be made into crisps (see Parsnip Crisps, page 110) and are excellent in pies and quiches. The skin is particularly nutritious; a simple, homey meal of jacket-baked sweet potatoes with an avocado, cos lettuce and toasted pine nut salad and a dish of steamed broccoli or cauliflower is colourful, tasty and good for you. For meat-eaters, the recipe here goes well with a roast of lamb.

curly Endive Salad with Walnuts

SERVES 8

olive oil for shallow frying
1 cup large cubes sourdough bread
salt
1 tablespoon white wine vinegar
freshly ground black pepper to taste
1 large clove garlic, crushed
3 tablespoons extra virgin olive oil
$\frac{1}{3}$ cup freshly shelled walnuts, roughly chopped
1 large curly endive, washed and dried and torn into bite-sized pieces
a handful of fresh basil leaves, torn into tiny pieces

Heat some olive oil in a small frying pan and when it is hot add the cubes of bread. Fry for 3–5 minutes, turning often with a slotted spoon, until evenly coloured. Transfer the bread cubes to a plate lined with absorbent kitchen paper, using the slotted spoon. Sprinkle with salt and leave to cool.

Mix the vinegar, $\frac{1}{4}$ teaspoon salt, black pepper and garlic together in a bowl. Whisk in the extra virgin olive oil. Add the walnuts, endive, basil leaves and croûtons. Toss well and leave for 5–10 minutes before serving; toss again just prior to serving.

Sweet Potatoes with Pine Nuts, Currants and Mint

chunks Hot Buttered Cucumber

SERVES 4–6

1 slim telegraph cucumber, washed and dried
large knob of butter
Maldon sea salt
freshly ground black pepper to taste
2 tablespoons snipped chives and a few chive
**   flowers if available**

Leave the skin on the cucumber if it is tender. Trim the ends and cut it into four or eight long strips (depending on the thickness). Slice off excess seeds, then cut the cucumber into chunks.

Heat a large frying pan over a medium-low heat and drop in the butter. Add the cucumber while the butter is sizzling and stirfry for a few minutes. Sprinkle with salt and grind on some black pepper. Continue cooking, stirring often, until the cucumber is hot (be careful not to let it fry). Sprinkle on the chives and chive flowers, if using, toss and serve immediately.

Hot cucumber *may seem a ridiculous idea at first glance, but it is the most superb vegetable to serve with a delicate grilled salmon steak – it's gorgeous! Tossing cucumber in hot butter seems to mute its indigestible properties. Salt, black pepper and chives add to the flavour and the pretty mauve petals of the flowers add to the charm.*

hunky Gratin of Winter Vegetables

SERVES 6

2 potatoes, peeled
1 small swede, peeled
2 carrots, peeled
3 parsnips, peeled (remove any woody cores)
1 celeriac, peeled
$\frac{1}{2}$ teaspoon salt
1 tablespoon chopped rosemary
freshly ground black pepper to taste
300ml cream
3 cloves garlic, crushed
$\frac{3}{4}$ cup water
butter

Slice all the vegetables very thinly. Put the potatoes in the bottom of a gratin dish and sprinkle a little salt and rosemary over them. Put the other vegetables in a large bowl, sprinkle with the rest of the salt and rosemary and grind on some black pepper. Toss well and turn into the gratin dish (it's advisable to keep the potatoes buried because they blacken if they are on top of the gratin).

Mix the cream, garlic and water together and pour over the vegetables. Dot the top of the vegetables with butter, cover with aluminium foil and cook for 40 minutes in an oven preheated to 180°C. Remove the foil and cook for 15 minutes more or until the vegetables are tender and lightly browned on top.

Garlic and cream *give this gratin a richness which makes it suitable as the main course of an all-vegetable meal. Serve it with a salad dressed with a vinaigrette of extra virgin olive oil, Dijon mustard, salt, black pepper and tarragon vinegar, and with lightly cooked broccoli. Alternatively, partner it with a big, hunky piece of roast beef, crusted with salt, black pepper and mustard, cooked until medium-rare, and a spinach salad.*

wild Porcini Mushroom Risotto

SERVES 4–6

25g dried porcini (or cèpe) mushrooms
300ml warm water
1 litre chicken or vegetable stock
2 tablespoons of olive oil
75g butter
1 small onion, finely chopped
1 clove garlic, crushed
$\frac{1}{2}$ cup dry red or white wine
400g Italian risotto rice (arborio, vialone nano or carnaroli)
$\frac{1}{4}$ teaspoon salt, or to taste
freshly ground black pepper to taste
a few gratings of fresh nutmeg
50g freshly grated Italian parmesan cheese, plus extra for serving

Put the porcini mushrooms in a bowl with the warm water and soak for 30 minutes. Reserving the soaking liquid, remove the mushrooms and rinse them well under running water. Chop them finely, discarding any woody bits. Strain the liquid into a bowl through a sieve lined with a piece of absorbent kitchen paper, then repeat the straining process.

Bring the stock to a low steady simmer, then lower the heat so that it stays hot but doesn't simmer (to avoid evaporation).

Choose a cast-iron casserole or heavy-based saucepan with a 3 litre capacity and set it over a moderate heat. Drop in the oil and half the butter, and add the onion and garlic. Sauté until a pale golden colour, then pour the wine in and cook until it has nearly evaporated.

Tip in the rice and sauté for 2 minutes until the rice is hot and coated with the butter and oil (don't let it fry or it will harden). Stir frequently with a wooden spoon, then stir in a ladleful of stock. This will evaporate quickly. Add a second ladleful of hot stock and stir gently but continuously until the stock has nearly evaporated. Continue adding stock and cooking in this way for 10–12 minutes, then add the prepared porcini. Heat the strained soaking liquid and start stirring it into the porcini, continuing to add more as it becomes absorbed. When it's all used up, use stock or water again.

The rice is ready when the grains are al dente; it will take around 20 minutes.

Stir in the salt, black pepper, nutmeg, the rest of the butter and the parmesan. Beat for 30 seconds then cover with a lid and leave to infuse for 1 minute. Serve with extra parmesan.

Porcini, or cèpe (Boletus edulis), *is an edible fungus, available fresh in some countries during autumn, or dried at other times of the year. Drying the porcini concentrates the woodsy aroma and savoury taste. Porcini give a deep mushroom flavour to any dish to which they are added.*

swirl Garbure Basque

SERVES 4

1 leek, chopped
1 large onion, sliced through the root then cut into slim wedges
6 cloves garlic, roughly chopped
2 stalks celery, roughly chopped
2 tablespoons olive oil
5 medium old potatoes, cut into chunks
2 carrots, cut into chunks
a handful (300g) of green beans, topped and tailed and cut into thirds
1 turnip, cut into chunks (optional)
2 large tomatoes, halved
2 litres water
1 teaspoon salt, or to taste
freshly ground black pepper to taste
2 tablespoons each chopped parsley and chopped chervil

Put the leek, onion, garlic and celery in a large saucepan with the oil, cover with a lid and cook gently for about 15 minutes or until tender; stir occasionally.

Add the rest of the vegetables and cook for 10 minutes, stirring occasionally. Pour in the water, add the salt and some black pepper and bring to the boil. Cover with a lid and cook gently for $2\frac{1}{2}$ hours, until the vegetables are fork-tender and breaking apart. Partially mash the vegetables with a potato masher, removing the tomato skins. Swirl the parsley and chervil in and check for seasoning. Serve hot.

This soup has a Basque accent, but, instead of the typical cabbage and white beans, it features green beans and is finished off with a handful of chopped chervil leaves, which introduce a pleasant aniseed flavour. If you are making the soup ahead of time, don't add the chervil and parsley until just prior to serving the soup because chervil, in particular, loses its flavour when heated.

Garbure Basque

grunt Leek, Bacon and Potato Soup

SERVES 8

1.8kg leeks
2 tablespoons olive oil
300g bacon, rind removed and chopped
1 large clove garlic, crushed
1kg waxy potatoes, peeled and cubed
freshly ground black pepper to taste
2 litres cold water
2 teaspoons salt
2 tablespoons coarsely chopped flat leaf parsley,
    plus extra for garnishing
1 tablespoon coarsely chopped mint

Trim the leeks, discarding coarse leaves, split lengthways, wash well and chop. Heat the oil in a large soup or stock pot over a medium heat until hot, then add the bacon. Brown well, letting it catch on the bottom of the pan a little. Add the leeks, garlic and potato and toss well to coat in the bacon fat. Put on a lid, lower the heat and cook gently for about 20 minutes, until the leeks are wilted; toss occasionally.

Grind on some black pepper, add the water and salt. Bring to a gentle boil, then simmer gently, partially covered, for 45–60 minutes, until the vegetables are very tender.

Let the soup cool for 15 minutes, then purée two-thirds of the mixture in a food processor or blender with the parsley. Mix with the unblended soup (this gives the soup a smooth body with chunky bits for interest).

Reheat until boiling, add the mint, then serve garnished with a little more chopped parsley.

I make versions of this soup all through winter, freezing any leftovers (this is a BIG pot of soup, which provides two meals for my family of four, but the recipe can be halved).

Blending the parsley with the soup gives the soup a pretty green hue. Adding bacon gives it more grunt, but it can be omitted if you don't eat meat. The mint gives the soup a fresh finish.

Leek, Bacon and Potato Soup

golden Potato Cake

SERVES 6

2kg old or all-purpose potatoes
75g butter, softened
salt

Peel the potatoes and slice very thinly into rounds. Butter a 25cm non-stick frying pan or heavy shallow dish that can go directly over the heat.

Cover the bottom of the pan with overlapping slices of potato, starting the first ring either around the outside edge of the pan or in the centre. Cover the entire bottom of the pan with circles of potato. This will be the presentation layer once the cake is turned out, so use the most even slices.

Lightly sprinkle with salt and dot with some butter. Continue in this way, layering potatoes, salt and butter, until all the potatoes are used. Tightly press a double thickness of aluminium foil around the edge of the pan, then cover with a lid (if the pan or container has no lid, cover with a heavy china plate).

Put the pan over a medium-low heat and cook for about 45 minutes or until the potatoes are tender and golden on the bottom. Take care with the heat; you should hear the potatoes sizzling gently and smell a glorious buttery smell during cooking.

Remove the pan from the heat and let the cake rest for 5 minutes. Remove the lid and foil, then loosen the potatoes carefully from the sides and bottom of the dish. Cover the pan with a large serving platter and carefully invert the potato cake onto the plate. Serve hot, cut into wedges.

Potatoes cooked slowly *in butter until crisp and golden are wickedly good. To try to alleviate some of the guilt associated with eating such a dish, forgo the perfect partner of savoury, salty rashers of crisp bacon (which really would be too much for the calorie counters) and serve it with a healthy watercress salad.*

Waxy new potatoes do not have enough sticky starch to hold the cooked cake together, so older ones are generally better, but I find the best result is with an all-purpose or mid-season potato, which has just enough starch to hold the cake together but not so much that the potato slices collapse and turn to fluff.

Potato Cake

cornerstone

fundamental

base

never

essential

trust

good to know

got to

reliable *primary*

foundation

Cauliflower Cheese

Red Peppered Cabbage

Roasted Carrots and Parsnips

Brussels Sprouts with Cream

Garlic Mash

Carrots and Parsnips in Chicken Stock

Gingered Broccoli

Green Beans with Garlic Butter

Oven-crisped Potatoes

Whipped Parsnips

Buttery Turnips

Roasties

Potato Purée

Buttered Jerusalem Artichokes

Parsnip and Swede Mash

fail

core

know

best-ever Cauliflower Cheese

SERVES 6–8

CHEESE SAUCE
2 level tablespoons butter
3 level tablespoons plain flour
300ml milk
$\frac{1}{4}$ teaspoon salt
2 tablespoons finely grated gruyère cheese

**1 medium cauliflower, washed and trimmed
    into florets**
salt

CRISP CRUMBS
**3 tablespoons (about 45g) butter, plus extra for
    greasing the bowl**
1 cup fresh breadcrumbs
a few pinches of salt
good grinding of black pepper
**2 tablespoons freshly grated Italian parmesan
    cheese**
1 tablespoon finely chopped parsley

First prepare the sauce. Melt the butter in a small saucepan, then remove the pan from the heat and add the flour. Blend well, then add the milk a third at a time, stirring well. Return the sauce to the heat, blend in the salt and stir constantly until it is boiling. Cook for 2 minutes, stirring, then remove it from the heat and beat in the gruyère cheese. Cover with a lid.

Plunge the cauliflower florets into a saucepan of boiling salted water and cook for 5 minutes. Drain, refresh with cold water, leave to drain again, then wrap in absorbent kitchen paper or a clean cloth to absorb clinging moisture.

Butter a small china basin of about 1 litre capacity. Put in the cauliflower florets, placing the stems pointing inwards and pressing them tightly together. Dribble about 3 tablespoons of the sauce over the stems as you layer up the cauliflower. Cover it with a small plate or saucer and put a weight on top.

Ten minutes before serving, tilt the bowl and drain off any accumulated liquid, then place the covered bowl in a hot oven to warm through. Gently heat the sauce (don't let it boil or it will go stringy). Invert the heated cauliflower onto a heated serving plate and spoon the hot sauce over. Scatter the crisp crumbs (instructions follow) over the top and serve immediately.

Crisp Crumbs

Heat a large frying pan and drop in the butter. When it is sizzling, add the breadcrumbs and cook over a medium heat, tossing often, until the crumbs are crisp and golden. Turn into a bowl and blend in the salt, black pepper, the parmesan and parsley. The crumbs will stay crisp for a few hours if they are left uncovered and stored at room temperature.

I know cheese sauce is anathema to some, but cauliflower cheese is one of those things I never grew out of. Here's a new slant on presenting it, although I still love it bubbling and crusty, gratinated with cheese on top.

In this recipe, the cauliflower is turned out so it looks like a whole cauliflower again. Generally I don't like to doctor food like this, but it makes boring old cauliflower look so much better. With cheese sauce and buttery crisp crumbs on top it looks so good it's impossible to stop delving into it!

stew Red Peppered Cabbage

SERVES 6

2 large knobs of butter
1 small onion, finely chopped
**1 red pepper (capsicum), cored, deseeded and
    finely chopped**
half a white or Savoy cabbage
$\frac{1}{2}$ teaspoon salt
freshly ground black pepper to taste
1 teaspoon finely chopped marjoram or oregano

Melt the butter in a large saucepan over a gentle heat and add the onion and red pepper. Cover with a lid and cook gently for about 10 minutes or until tender.

Meanwhile, prepare the cabbage by cutting it in half and cutting out the hard core. Shred the leaves finely and add to the pan. Toss well and add the salt and black pepper and the chosen herb. Continue cooking, tossing constantly, until the cabbage just starts to wilt (about 4 minutes). Immediately tip it into a heated dish and serve.

Cauliflower Cheese

roots Roasted Carrots and Parsnips

SERVES 4

4–8 slim parsnips, peeled and trimmed
4–8 long thin carrots, peeled and trimmed
1½ tablespoons extra virgin olive oil
1 teaspoon chopped rosemary
freshly ground black pepper to taste
Maldon sea salt

If the parsnips or carrots are large, cut in half lengthways. Mix the oil, rosemary, black pepper and a few pinches of salt together in a bowl, then rub the mixture over the vegetables.

Put the vegetables in a shallow oven dish or on a baking tray. Bake for about 30 minutes or until tender and golden, in an oven preheated to 220°C; turn the vegetables during cooking. Serve immediately.

Carrots are one *of the best vegetables to roast because roasting intensifies their sweetness without turning them candy-sweet. Parsnips and rosemary are one of those matches which make the nostrils twitch and the palate sing. If you're a meat-eater, a big, hunky piece of roasted beef is superb with these vegetables. For vegetarians, they go with Brussels sprouts in cream, stuffed tomatoes, spinach salad, green beans, almost anything!*

shake Brussels Sprouts with Cream

SERVES 4

500g young Brussels sprouts
salt
100ml cream
freshly ground black pepper to taste
freshly grated nutmeg to taste

Trim the sprouts and remove any damaged leaves. Cut a shallow cross on the bottom of each. Wash well. Plunge the sprouts into a saucepan of boiling, lightly salted water and cook, uncovered, for about 5 minutes or until crunch-tender (or cook to your liking). Drain and let the cold tap run over them until they are cool. Then shake them well and turn them onto absorbent kitchen paper to dry.

Put the cream in a saucepan and reduce it by half over a medium heat. Add some black pepper and nutmeg and put in the Brussels sprouts. Shake well and simmer gently for a few minutes until they are heated through. Turn into a heated dish and serve immediately.

Some of the old *methods of food preparation are a mystery to us, but others remain very practical. Cutting a cross on the bottom of Brussels sprouts, for instance, does serve a purpose. It allows the boiling water to enter the base of the sprouts, the densest part, ensuring it is cooked by the time the rest of the leaves are. It's particularly helpful with more mature sprouts, which can become soggy on the outside before the centre is tender.*

cure-all Garlic Mash

SERVES 4–6

2 heads of garlic, peeled
250ml dry white wine or chicken stock
1½ tablespoons extra virgin olive oil
pinch of salt
freshly ground black pepper to taste

Put the cloves of garlic in a small saucepan with the wine or stock. Bring to a gentle boil and cook gently until tender and all the liquid is absorbed. Mash with a fork, add the oil and season to taste with salt and black pepper.

Store covered and refrigerated; use within 24 hours.

Serve the garlic mash *on steaks or with seafood or chicken. It's also great spread on toasted focaccia or bread and topped with salad ingredients and cold chicken, or lettuce, bacon, avocado and tomato. Vegetarians should try the mash on jacket-baked potatoes.*

The health benefits *and 'cure-all' claims about garlic are substantial. It is reputedly good for the intestines, is said to lower high blood pressure and a heavy dose of it has been known to clear up a bad case of pimples (pity about the breath). It is widely believed to build up resistance to infection and, contrary to what many people say ('garlic repeats on me'), garlic aids digestion.*

The most enduring claim is that of its antiseptic properties. It is the sulphide that apparently does the trick. In the First World War, the raw juice was used extensively on wounds to prevent them turning septic.

If garlic is stored in a moist place, it will start to sprout. The green sprout is strong tasting and is the culprit, I believe, for garlic 'repeating' on you later. It is easily removed by cutting the garlic in half and picking it out with the point of a sharp knife. Old and yellowing garlic should be thrown out. It will taste sour and can ruin a dish, especially if used raw.

If making garlic vinegar, garlic oil or long-keeping marinades, do not rely on the vinegar, salt or oil content alone to preserve them. Garlic needs to be properly blanched to ensure all the enzymes are inactivated. You should think twice before buying garlic pickles and preserves if the product does not contain a preservative. The garlic may look harmless but, if it has been used raw, there is a potential danger of botulism.

simmer Carrots and Parsnips in Chicken Stock

SERVES 6

600g (6 slim) carrots, peeled
600g (4 medium) parsnips, peeled
50g butter
¼ teaspoon salt
¼ cup chicken stock
freshly ground black pepper to taste
2 tablespoons chopped chervil (optional)

Slice the carrots and parsnips into thin sticks or elongated rounds, discarding any woody cores in the parsnips. Melt the butter in a saucepan and put the carrots in first, then the parsnips (the parsnips cook more quickly than the carrots and are better on the top).

Add the salt and chicken stock, cover the pan with a lid and bring to a gentle boil. Immediately lower the heat, then cook very gently for about 25 minutes or until tender. If there is a lot of juice in the pan, increase the heat and drive it off. Grind a little black pepper over and turn into a heated serving dish. Scatter the chervil over, if using, and serve immediately. A great plate mate for roast lamb.

To make this *dish suitable for vegetarians, use vegetable stock.*

hot wok Gingered Broccoli

SERVES 6

700–800g (2 heads) broccoli, trimmed into florets
salt
1 tablespoon olive oil
small piece of fresh ginger, peeled and finely
  grated (if very fibrous, squeeze out the juice and
  use it without the fibre)
$\frac{1}{4}$ cup water
1 tablespoon soy sauce
1 tablespoon dry sherry
1 teaspoon raw sugar

Either steam the broccoli or boil it gently in salted water – a few minutes should do it. Rinse the broccoli in plenty of cold water until it feels cool, then dry it on absorbent kitchen paper; this can be done in advance.

About 5 minutes before serving time, heat a large frying pan or wok and add the oil. When it is hottish add the ginger and stirfry for 1 minute, then add the broccoli. Cook for 1 minute, tossing gently. Mix and add the water, soy sauce, sherry and raw sugar. Cook, stirring often, for 1–2 minutes, until the broccoli is heated through. Transfer to a heated serving dish and serve immediately.

Do not buy anything but the freshest broccoli. If it is limp or starting to go yellow, it's dead and nutritionally depleted. But it's worth eating lots of fresh broccoli – it's got a big whack of Vitamin C, plus Vitamin K, helps bump up the calcium intake, contains iron and potassium, and, it is claimed, it prevents some cancers.

Fresh broccoli, steamed or blanched, is a delight to eat. If you start to smell broccoli when it is cooking – a sulphurous smell as opposed to a sort of green vegetable smell (a little bit bitter in the nostrils, like a cut green pepper), it is overcooked. Drain it immediately and cool it quickly in cold water to try to rescue it. Once it starts to smell, it's on a downward slide and loses its good fresh taste. But you can safely blanch it ahead of time and finish it off any way you like.

Broccoli takes well to Asian flavourings, to garlic and to herbs. And here's an Italian idea that has to be tried to be believed – it's the only time I would cook broccoli until really tender (add a fresh bay leaf to the water to sweeten the air, and open the windows!). Mash cooked broccoli florets in a saucepan with loads of crushed garlic and extra virgin olive oil. It is extraordinary.

garlicky Green Beans with Garlic Butter

SERVES 6

300g slim green beans, topped and tailed
salt
knob of butter
1 clove garlic, finely crushed
freshly ground black pepper to taste

Plunge the beans into a saucepan of gently boiling salted water. Cook uncovered for 3–5 minutes or until crisp-tender. Drain and refresh with a cup of cold water.

Wipe out the pan, drop in the butter and add the garlic. Set over a gentle heat and add the beans. Grind on some black pepper and leave on the heat until hot, tossing often. Tip into a heated serving dish, with all the garlicky buttery bits. Serve immediately.

bliss Oven-crisped Potatoes

SERVES 6

1.5kg (6 large) old floury potatoes or potatoes
  which are good for roasting
$\frac{1}{4}$ cup olive oil
salt

Peel the potatoes and slice thinly by hand or in the food processor. Turn the sliced potatoes into a large, shallow ovenproof dish and drizzle with oil. Rub the oil through the potatoes, making sure each slice is well coated with oil. Spread them out evenly then sprinkle generously with salt. Cook in an oven preheated to 200°C for 1 hour or until wonderfully crisp and golden.

I've recommended old potatoes for this because the high starch content ensures that they will brown and crisp well. But I've made a good job of them with freshly dug all-purpose potatoes, too. These potatoes are no fuss, but resist the urge to turn them during cooking because the crusty bits which catch in the dish are part of the appeal.

Oven-crisped Potatoes

creamed Whipped Parsnips

SERVES 4–6

1kg parsnips, peeled and trimmed
salt
large knob of butter
freshly ground black pepper to taste
200ml milk, brought to boiling point
chopped parsley for garnishing

Cut the parsnips into slim wedges, discarding any woody centres. Put them in a large saucepan and cover with cold water. Sprinkle with salt and bring to the boil. Cook gently, partially covered with a lid, for 12–15 minutes or until very tender; remove any scum that rises to the surface. Drain, and rinse with warm water, then purée the parsnips in a food processor or mash them with a potato masher.

Beat in the butter, 1 teaspoon of salt and a little black pepper. Beat in enough of the hot milk (150–200ml) to make the purée light and creamy. If you are using a food processor, the whole operation can be carried out in the processor bowl.

Transfer the purée to a heated serving dish, sprinkle with parsley and serve hot.

The purée can be prepared ahead and reheated over a low heat; you may need a little extra hot milk, and you'll need to stir it constantly.

If the sweet *woodsy earthy taste of parsnips is an acquired taste, then it's a taste I acquired quite young. I always loved them emerging deeply golden and aromatic from the oven around a joint of roast meat, and I sought out chunks of them in my mother's famous vegetable soup. Whipping parsnips with salt, black pepper, butter and hot milk transforms them into a milder vegetable which can act as a cushion under sauced foods or roasted meats and gravy – a good contrast to a platter of crisp snappy vegetables.*

Rosemary and garlic rubbed into beef or lamb before roasting makes a glorious match for whipped parsnips.

Alternatively, for an all-vegetable meal, use the whipped parsnips as a cushion for a colourful stirfry of assorted vegetables well flavoured with fresh herbs and garlic. Balance the meal with a mushroom dish.

crisp Buttery Turnips

SERVES 6

800g small white turnips, peeled (if bigger than
egg-sized, cut into quarters)
salt
1 tablespoon oil
50g butter
1 medium onion, finely chopped
4 tablespoons fresh breadcrumbs
freshly ground black pepper to taste
1 tablespoon finely chopped parsley

Put the turnips in a saucepan, cover with cold water, salt lightly and bring to the boil. Boil for 1 minute, then drain. Dry on absorbent kitchen paper.

Put the oil and two-thirds of the butter in a frying pan and set over a medium heat. When sizzling, add the onion and cook, stirring often, for about 10 minutes or until lightly browned (take care not to let it burn). Add the breadcrumbs and the remaining butter and season with $\frac{1}{4}$ teaspoon of salt and some black pepper. Cook, tossing often, until crisp, then add the turnips to the pan and cook for 5 minutes or until heated through. Blend in the parsley, then turn into a heated serving dish (include all the crispy bits). Serve immediately.

The best advice *I can give regarding turnips is to buy small ones only, because they will be much sweeter and more peppery in flavour without any strong aromas and taste. Buy them when they are very fresh and use them straight away. This way the turnip is a thoroughly well-behaved vegetable. If they are spanking fresh, they don't even need peeling, just give them a good wash. They can be used in soups and casseroles, and they glaze beautifully in a little butter and sugar. They can also be roasted and are good in mixed vegetable dishes too. The French take great care in growing turnips and pick them young and fresh. The English, on the other hand, have a reputation for growing large, coarse strong-tasting turnips, which no amount of seasonings and butter can mute. Turnips contain Vitamin C and a good dollop of calcium.*

scratch Roasties

SERVES 6–8

1.5kg old potatoes, suitable for roasting
salt
90ml vegetable oil

Peel the potatoes, cut them into large chunks, then put them in a saucepan. Salt lightly and bring to the boil.

Meanwhile, heat the oil in a roasting tin in a hot oven.

Cook the potatoes, uncovered, for 5 minutes, then drain well. As soon as the potatoes are cool enough to handle, scratch them all over with a fork. This makes a rough layer that crumbles and crisps well.

When the oil is very hot and just starting to haze, remove the roasting tin from the oven. Put in the potatoes, in one layer. Cook for about $1\frac{1}{4}$–$1\frac{1}{2}$ hours, in an oven preheated to 200°C, turning them from time to time. Sprinkle with salt during the last 15 minutes. When they are crisp and crunchy, transfer them to a plate lined with absorbent kitchen paper. Drain briefly, then move them to a heated serving plate. Serve immediately.

Older potatoes are best *for roasting because the high starch content gives a fluffier inside and a crisper crunch to the outside. Choose potatoes of an even size so they cook through at the same time. Parboiling the potatoes, then scratching the surfaces with a fork, is an old Cordon Bleu trick – but one which I use often. If potatoes with smooth surfaces sit in hot fat (oil or whatever) they tend to absorb it, but if the surfaces are a little rough, scratched and ridged as it were, a little air passes underneath, they don't sit in the fat and absorb it. The result? Better roast potatoes!*

If the potatoes are too crowded, sitting one on top of the other, moisture will be trapped in and they won't brown. If this is your only option (on holiday, for example, or cooking for crowds), set the heat on maximum and just let the tops crisp, then turn them over with a fish slice and crisp the bottoms – camping-style 'roast' potatoes!

whipped Potato Purée

Ever wondered how to get a fluffy, light potato purée? Start by peeling the potatoes and cutting them into smallish, even-sized cubes; this way they will cook quickly and evenly and not become water-logged.

Put the potatoes in a large saucepan and cover them generously with cold water. Add some salt, then boil gently until tender. Drain well and return to the saucepan. Put the saucepan back over the heat for 30 seconds (without the lid); this drives off any clinging moisture, making the potatoes drier and improving the flavour (be careful not to scorch them though, or the flavour will be ruined).

Mash with a hand masher or pass through a mouli-légumes; a food processor makes them heavy and sticky. Heat a small amount of milk until just under boiling point (use as much as necessary to make a soft purée). Add to the purée a little at a time, along with a knob of butter, beating well with a wooden spoon; hot milk makes the purée fluffy, cold milk added to a starchy vegetable makes it tacky and gluey. Hot milk also stops the purée turning greyish, and, of course, keeps it hot. Beating it by hand introduces air and keeps the purée light.

Check the seasoning, add salt, beat it in, then taste and continue adding more salt until the purée has a pronounced 'potato' flavour. It should taste delicious.

The purée is best served immediately, but if you do have to hold it for a time, don't keep it over heat; it will collapse, turn watery and grey, and lose its goodness and good taste. Better to remove it from the heat, pour a little hot milk over the surface to prevent it from drying out, and leave it to cool. Reheat over a gentle heat, beating with a wooden spoon, adding more hot milk if necessary.

earthy Buttered Jerusalem Artichokes

SERVES 4

1kg large, even-shaped Jerusalem artichokes, scrubbed
1 tablespoon lemon juice
salt
30g butter
freshly ground black pepper to taste
1 tablespoon chopped parsley

Put the Jerusalem artichokes in a saucepan and cover with cold water. Add the lemon juice and a few pinches of salt, cover with a lid and quickly bring to the boil. Immediately reduce the heat to low and cook, partially covered with a lid, until the Jerusalem artichokes are just tender (5–12 minutes, depending on the size). Drain in a colander, peel with a small sharp knife, and cut into thinnish rounds; they may be prepared an hour or so ahead to this point.

When you are ready to finish them off, heat the butter in a large frying pan over a medium heat and when sizzling add them to the pan. Stir to coat in the butter, seasoning well with salt and black pepper.

Cook over a medium heat for 4–5 minutes, stirring often. (If you prefer them crisper, fry them in the butter for 10–12 minutes or until crisp.) When well heated through stir in the parsley. Transfer to a heated dish and serve immediately.

Jerusalem artichokes, a tuber native to North America, look like gnarled pieces of fresh ginger and have an interesting, nutty-earthy flavour with just a hint of sourness. They are not related to globe artichokes, but some say there is a similarity of taste (I've never detected it). They can be made into a soup, sautéed, baked, sauced, turned into fritters, 'souffléed', soused in a vinaigrette, or used raw in salads.

They tend to darken once peeled or cut, but putting them in either acidulated water (water to which has been added some form of acid, such as lemon juice) or milk, lessens the discolouration.

crush Parsnip and Swede Mash

SERVES 6 OR MORE

800g (approximately 5 medium) parsnips, peeled
450g (2 small) swedes, peeled
butter
salt
freshly ground black pepper to taste
snipped chives

Cut the parsnips and swedes into chunks. Steam or boil them separately until they are very tender, then return them to the dry pan and set back on the heat briefly to dry. Mash with a potato masher, mixing in as much butter as you dare, along with good amounts of salt, black pepper and chives. Serve immediately with a lump of melting butter on top.

Swedes and parsnips are not the most popular vegetables. Some people think of swedes as fit only for cattle fodder, and parsnips are another hard sell. But they can be delicious – you just have to know how to deal with them. Mashed into submission with plenty of seasoning and loads of butter they are positively charming! Flop them into a hot bowl, fluff them up with a fork, stick a lump of butter in the centre and serve them with a roasted rack of lamb imbued with rosemary and perfumed with orange zest.

In Sweden (and also in the US), swedes are known as rutabaga, which translates as 'red bags', and refers to the crowns of the vegetables, which are tinged with a purpley-red colour. Swedes and turnips are closely related, but the leaves of swede plants are not eaten because they are too fibrous, even when young; young turnip leaves are often served as a green vegetable. The flesh is similar to turnip, a little coarse, not smooth like a potato, and is pinky-yellow in colour, becoming orange-yellow after cooking.

Although swedes are available most of the year, the texture and taste of them improves once the vegetables have experienced a good frost, making them an excellent, and inexpensive, winter vegetable.

Young, freshly picked swedes are crisp and sweet and can be eaten raw as part of a crudité selection. Swedes are thought to help fight cancers. They contain traces of antioxidant vitamins beta-carotene and C. They are also a good source of fibre.

weights & measures

In New Zealand, South Africa, the USA and in England 1 tablespoon equals 15ml. In Australia, 1 tablespoon equals 20ml.

These variations will not adversely affect the end result, as long as the same spoon is used consistently, so the proportions are correct.

Grams to Ounces and vice versa

General			Exact		
30g	=	1oz	1oz	=	28.35g
60g	=	2oz	2oz	=	56.70g
90g	=	3oz	3oz	=	85.05g
120g	=	4oz	4oz	=	113.04g
150g	=	5oz	5oz	=	141.08g
180g	=	6oz	6oz	=	170.01g
210g	=	7oz	7oz	=	198.04g
230g	=	8oz	8oz	=	226.08g
260g	=	9oz	9oz	=	255.01g
290g	=	10oz	10oz	=	283.05g
320g	=	11oz	11oz	=	311.08g
350g	=	12oz	12oz	=	340.02g
380g	=	13oz	13oz	=	368.05g
410g	=	14oz	14oz	=	396.09g
440g	=	15oz	15oz	=	425.02g
470g	=	16oz	16oz	=	453.06g

Recipes based on these (International Units) rounded values

Liquid Measurements

25ml	(28.4ml)	=	1fl oz				
150ml	(142ml)	=	5fl oz	=	$\frac{1}{4}$ pint	=	1 gill
275ml	(284ml)	=	10fl oz	=	$\frac{1}{2}$ pint		
425ml	(426ml)	=	15fl oz	=	$\frac{3}{4}$ pint		
575ml	(568ml)	=	20fl oz	=	1 pint		

Spoon Measures

$\frac{1}{4}$ teaspoon	=	1.25ml
$\frac{1}{2}$ teaspoon	=	2.5ml
1 teaspoon	=	5ml
1 tablespoon	=	15ml

In NZ, SA, USA and UK 1 tablespoon = 15ml

In Australia 1 tablespoon = 20ml

1 tablespoon butter equals about 10g

Measurements
cm to approx inches

0.5cm	=	$\frac{1}{4}''$	5cm	=	2″
1.25cm	=	$\frac{1}{2}''$	7.5cm	=	3″
2.5cm	=	1″	10cm	=	4″

Cake Tin Sizes
cm to approx inches

15cm	=	6″	23cm	=	9″
18cm	=	7″	25cm	=	10″
20cm	=	8″			

Alternative names

cake tin	cake/baking pan
capsicum/pepper	sweet bell pepper
coriander	cilantro
cornflour	cornstarch
eggplant	aubergine
essence	extract
frying pan	skillet
grill	broil
hard-boiled egg	hard-cooked egg
icing sugar	confectioner's sugar
king prawns	jumbo shrimps/scampi
kumara	sweet potato
minced meat	ground meat
pawpaw	papaya
rock melon	cantaloupe
seed	pip
spring onion	scallion/green onion
zucchini	courgette

Oven Temperatures
Celsius to Fahrenheit

110°C	225°F	very cool
130°C	250°F	
140°C	275°F	cool
150°C	300°F	
170°C	325°F	warm
180°C	350°F	moderate
190°C	375°F	fairly hot
200°C	400°F	
220°C	425°F	hot
230°C	450°F	very hot
240°C	475°F	

Abbreviations

g	gram
kg	kilogram
mm	millimetre
cm	centimetre
ml	millilitre
°C	degrees Celsius
°F	degrees Fahrenheit

American–Imperial

in	inch
lb	pound
oz	ounce

index

acknowledgements

The support from the New Holland Publishing Group, including the Australian and English companies, deserves acknowledgement but in particular I'd like to single out Renée Lang, Belinda Cooke, Yvonne Thomson and Andrew Rumbles from the New Zealand office. They've done a sterling job.

Thanks to my literary agent of 13 years, Ray Richards.

I've been lucky to have my favourite team assembled again to work on *Fresh*. A big thanks to Barbara Nielsen, my editor, who manages to bring out the best in me, and Christine Hansen, who has done a cracking job of the design. I'm thrilled with the photography by Ian Batchelor. He's simply the best!

Heaps of thanks to Remo, my husband. He had to do a little more than eat the recipe tests this time. His help with food styling was terrific.

I'd also like to thank Julie Dalzell, publisher of *Cuisine* magazine, and Barb Rogers, editor of 'Viva' (the *New Zealand Herald's* lifestyle supplement). These two women have been a wonderful help to me in my career.

A big thanks to:

Milly's of Ponsonby
Auckland, New Zealand
Tel. 64 9 376-1550

Country Road
Auckland, New Zealand
Tel. 64 9 524-9685